WALKING DICKENS' LONDON

LEE JACKSON

SHIRE PUBLICATIONS

Published in Great Britain in 2012 by Shire Publications Ltd,
Midland House, West Way, Botley, Oxford OX2 0PH, United Kingdom.
44-02 23rd Street, Suite 219, Long Island City, NY 11101, USA.

E-mail: shire@shirebooks.co.uk   www.shirebooks.co.uk

A CIP catalogue record for this book is available from the British Library.

Shire General no. 3.   ISBN-13: 978 0 74781 134 3

Lee Jackson has asserted his right under the Copyright, Designs and Patents Act, 1988, to be identified
as the author of this book.

Designed by Myriam Bell Design and typeset in Perpetua and Calibri.
Maps by Nick Rowland.
Printed in China through Worldprint Ltd.

12 13 14 15 16   10 9 8 7 6 5 4 3 2 1

ACKNOWLEDGEMENTS

I would like to offer my most sincere thanks to the following kind individuals, who volunteered to test
some of the walks or offered their help and advice. Their support was much appreciated. If I have
missed anyone from this list, please do accept my most sincere apologies.

Rob Baker (Archivist of the RSA), Sue Bailey, Osian Barnes, Louise Brown, Lewina Coote, Rachel
Craven, James Doeser, John Edwards from London Tavern Trails, Charlotte Elliston, Leigh Francis,
Hazel Ingrey, Holly Kosmin, Julia Lee, John Levin, Rose McNamee, Dean Peters, Martin Slade, Sarah
Slade, Vida Starcevic, Andy Stone, Louie Stowell, Peter Stubley, Mischa van den Brandhof, Bruno
Vincent, Eley Williams, Sarah Young.

Copyright holders are acknowledged as follows: the Carlton Club library, page 12 (top); courtesy of
Ken Reid, page 16 (top); courtesy of the Wallace Collection, page 18.

Out-of-copyright sources are acknowledged as follows: Mayhew & Binny, *The Criminal Prisons of London*,
1862, page 97; George Birch, *The Descriptive Album of London*, *c*.1896, pages 15, 51, 52, 80; 'London
Edition' of *Dickens' works* (Caxton Publishing Co., *c*.1902), pages 5, 7, 21, 29, 31, 59, 63, 66, 70, 76, 79,
82, 87, 88, 95, 108, 110, 120, 132; *Old and New London* (Cassell Petter & Galpin, *c*.1892), pages 10,
31, 34, 42, 46, 58, 61, 73, 83, 85, 94, 114, 125, 127; *Punch*, 1857, page 25; *The Queen's London: a
Pictorial and Descriptive Record of the Streets, Buildings, Parks and Scenery of the Great Metropolis*, 1896, pages
16, 130; *Sketches of London Life and Character*, 1849, pages 20, 36.

Photographs from author's collection, pages 101, 105, 107, 118.

CONTENTS

Introduction   4

Walk 1: St James's and Mayfair   9

Walk 2: Soho and Covent Garden   23

Walk 3: The Strand and Fleet Street   40

Walk 4: Bloomsbury and King's Cross   56

Walk 5: Holborn   71

Walk 6: Clerkenwell   85

Walk 7: St Paul's and Borough   99

Walk 8: City and Riverside   115

Index   134

INTRODUCTION

'So you were never in London before?' said Mr Wemmick to me.
'No,' said I.
'I was new here once,' said Mr Wemmick. 'Rum to think of now!'
'You are well acquainted with it now?'
'Why, yes,' said Mr Wemmick. 'I know the moves of it.'

Great Expectations

I ADMIRE THE DICKENSIAN IDEA that one comes to 'know the moves' of London. It implies a shifting, evasive opponent, which somehow must be wrestled into submission – a city that will attempt to fox and confuse the casual stranger. The implication is almost that London can never be truly 'known'. Nonetheless, this guide presents eight walks through the heart of Dickens' London, which will, at the very least, put you in a similar position to Mr Wemmick. The book is intended to be both compact and specific. All the walks, with one exception, take place entirely within central London; and I have included various references to Dickens' life, characters in his novels, and pieces of his journalism. As well as famous locations, historic pubs and quirky museums, this guide will direct you to obscure landmarks that are not part of the standard tourist trail; it will set you wandering through neglected courtyards and alleys, from the West End to the City of London, and along the river Thames. Moreover, while I will point out where particular buildings once stood, you should also discover many aspects of the Victorian metropolis surviving in modern London.

DICKENS COMES TO LONDON

Charles Dickens, the son of John Dickens, an assistant clerk in the Navy Pay Office, was born in Portsmouth on 7 February 1812. John's employers periodically moved him from one location to another, and Charles' early childhood was spent in Portsmouth, London, Sheerness and Chatham. The family returned to London in 1822, when John was recalled to Somerset House on the Strand. This was the young author's proper introduction to the 'great metropolis' and it was a difficult time. For a short period the family lived on the borders of respectability in Bayham Street, Camden, a lower-middle class district. John, however, struggled with mounting debts and was committed to the Marshalsea debtors' prison in 1824. The young Charles, meanwhile, was obliged to leave his schooling and go to work, labelling pots of boot-black at Warren's blacking factory. Both of these episodes left a profound mark on the author.

John Dickens left prison after only three months, helped by a fortuitous legacy, and Charles was eventually returned to education. Yet the fortunes of the Dickens family were hardly settled, and as a result of another financial crisis in 1827 Charles again had to find employment. He began work as a solicitor's clerk in Gray's Inn and found the job profoundly unsatisfying. Consequently, the following year, he embarked on a career as a journalist, teaching himself shorthand – an early sign of his determination and restless ambition – and began working as a freelance reporter in the law courts of Doctors' Commons. He then moved on to reporting on parliamentary affairs. His first piece of published fiction was in the *Monthly Magazine* in 1833,

Charles Dickens in 1868.

but he continued working as a journalist and even toyed with the idea of becoming either a barrister or an actor. While at the *Morning Chronicle* newspaper in 1834 he began writing a series of pieces on London life, many in a humorous vein, which would be collected together in 1836 as *Sketches by Boz*. He then created the character of Mr Pickwick, after a commission from the newly founded publishers Chapman & Hall. The story's first number was published in March 1836. *The Pickwick Papers* was an immediate and roaring success. *Oliver Twist* and *Nicholas Nickleby* followed in swift succession. By the end of the 1830s Dickens was already an established star of the nineteenth-century literary firmament and would remain in that exalted position until his death in 1870.

THE CHARACTER OF DICKENS' LONDON

This book takes you on eight tours of the streets that Dickens himself walked and shows you some of the buildings and sights that featured in his life and work. Nevertheless, as you walk through the city, you will have to use your imagination and make several adjustments if you wish to picture it in its early Victorian heyday.

Dickens' London was, above all, a gloomier city. Fog, heavy with pollution from domestic coal fires and the factory chimneys of the South Bank, could shroud the whole capital in darkness. At night link-boys carried flaming torches, hoping for a tip of a few pennies, to guide the wealthy back to their homes. Gas was introduced in the 1810s, but not universally taken up. While London's shops competed over ever increasing displays of plate glass, illuminated by dozens of gas jets, the proprietor of the Haymarket Theatre ('in consequence of some absurd prejudice') ignored his rivals and stuck to oil lamps until 1853. The brightness of electric lighting did not begin to supersede the flickering yellow glow of gas until the last decades of the century.

Fog was not merely a visual phenomenon. It 'smutted' the clothing and left the throat sore, inflaming lung complaints. When the winter fogs subsided, there were other hazards: dried horse dung filled the streets in the summer and turned into a noxious airborne dust. Parishes sent round water-carts to spray the main thoroughfares, and crossing-sweepers would clear a path from one side of a road to the other, but the roads were generally rather foul and messy. Cobbles were being replaced by other forms of paving, but the principal method was using 'macadam' – small chunks of stone pummelled down into a flat layer – which was often loosened and dug out by the passage of carriage wheels, adding to the filth on the streets.

Although we perhaps have an idea of a typical 'Victorian' street, the buildings of Dickens' London were not of one homogenous style. Among carefully planned Georgian squares and terraces, and newer developments, there were still many survivals from previous eras, and also many slum dwellings. These were generally old houses in varying states of decay rather than purpose-built shanties, although both could be found. Likewise, when we think of Victorian public buildings, we tend to picture the dramatic Victorian Gothic that

An original manuscript page from *David Copperfield*.

flourished from the mid-century, for example the Midland Grand Hotel, built in the late 1860s. Most public buildings of Dickens' time, however, were neo-classical or Italianate in style. We shall see both types of architecture in our walks.

What this book can never show you is the people: wealthy men in stove-pipe hats and silk suits; the more dandified 'fast' sorts with colourful waistcoats and jewelled tie-pins; poorer men dressed in coarse cotton fustian; well-to-do women in various sizes of crinoline, according to the year and the fashion; working-class girls parading a handful of feathers or ribbons, or a particular kind of bonnet, to compete in style. These are the people whom you will meet only in Dickens' writing. You may, at least, use this guide to stroll in their footsteps.

CHOOSE YOUR WALK

This book contains eight walks through central London, all of which can be finished within one or two hours (see each walk for further guidance as to timings). The first is through *St James's and Mayfair*, the most aristocratic part of the Victorian capital – the district of the gentlemen's club and the palatial town-house. Next is *Soho and Covent Garden*, incorporating the slum-ridden 'rookery' of Seven Dials and the bustle of Covent Garden market. The *Strand and Fleet Street* walk leads you along the principal route between Westminster and the City to the spot that marks the commencement of the author's career. The *Bloomsbury and King's Cross* walk begins with one of Dickens' earliest homes in the capital, often overlooked, and proceeds on a grand tour of the district that he twice made his home. The *Holborn* walk incorporates much of legal London, known to Dickens as a young clerk. The *Clerkenwell* walk takes you from the slums of Field Lane to a hanging at Newgate. The *St Paul's and Borough* walk begins with the great cathedral and crosses the river to the coaching inns of Borough High Street and the ruins of the Marshalsea prison. Finally, the *City and Riverside* walk commences in the heart of the City of London and winds along the banks of the Thames, through the maritime heart of the Victorian docks.

Whether you take one or all of these strolls through London's past, I hope each contains something novel and informative. I increasingly find myself spotting pieces of Dickens' London lurking amid the clutter of modern life, whether it is the glimpse of an old gaslight or a fading street-sign. The art of the dedicated time-traveller is to start putting them together – and these walks are one way to begin.

Lee Jackson, 2011

WALK 1:
ST JAMES'S AND MAYFAIR

Starting location: Horse Guards Parade, SW1A 2AX.

Nearest tube station: Westminster or St James's Park.

Walking time: 1¼ to 1½ hours.

Opening hours and alternative routes:

- ST JAMES'S CHURCH, Piccadilly: daily, 8 a.m. to 6.30 p.m. (although may not be accessible during events such as concerts or weddings). *If the church is closed, there is a path immediately adjoining (called Church Place) which will take you from Jermyn Street to Piccadilly.*

- BURLINGTON ARCADE: Monday to Wednesday, 8 a.m. to 6.30 p.m.; Thursday, 8 a.m. to 7 p.m.; Friday, 8 a.m. to 6.30 p.m.; Saturday, 9 a.m. to 6.30 p.m.; Sunday, 11 a.m. to 5 p.m. *If the Arcade is shut, use Old Bond Street, which runs parallel to the Arcade, and turn right into Burlington Gardens.*

- WALLACE COLLECTION: daily, 10 a.m. to 5 p.m.

  N.B. Opening hours may vary during public holidays.

HORSE GUARDS PARADE and the Palladian architecture of the Horse Guards building (built 1750–8), the official gateway to both St James's and Buckingham Palace, provide a grand location from which to commence our first walk, through the wealthiest part of Dickens' London.

Guardsmen have stood sentry on this spot since the restoration of the monarchy in 1660. Yet the average Victorian would have crossed the Parade not only to admire these worthy defenders of the throne (Peggotty takes Mr Dick to see them in *David Copperfield*) but for another purpose: to find the correct time. The Horse Guards clock, atop the building, was famous as the most accurate

in London, until the erection in 1859 of Parliament's 'Big Ben'. Mark Tapley attends to its chimes in *Martin Chuzzlewit* and Dickens refers to 'Half past five, p.m., Horse Guards' time' in *Bleak House*. Off-duty guardsmen would often stroll in nearby St James's Park, beset by admirers, particularly the nursemaids who took their young charges to enjoy the park's salubrious open spaces.

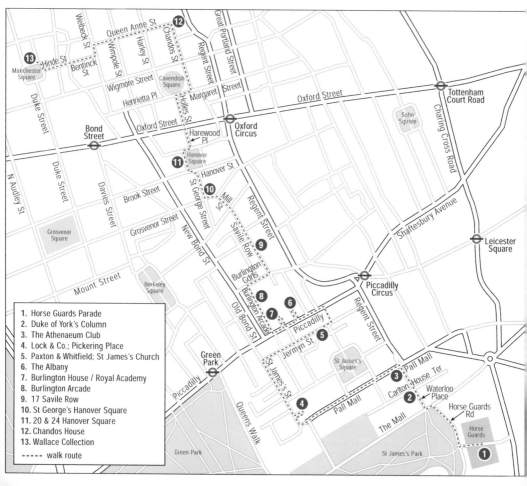

1. Horse Guards Parade
2. Duke of York's Column
3. The Athenaeum Club
4. Lock & Co.; Pickering Place
5. Paxton & Whitfield; St James's Church
6. The Albany
7. Burlington House / Royal Academy
8. Burlington Arcade
9. 17 Savile Row
10. St George's Hanover Square
11. 20 & 24 Hanover Square
12. Chandos House
13. Wallace Collection

----- walk route

Far left: A trooper from the Life Guards, part of the Household Cavalry.

Left: Frederick, Duke of York and Albany (1763–1827).

Opposite top: Fresh milk, curds and whey were sold from stalls in St James's Park.

As you walk up Horse Guards Road towards the Duke of York's column, try to picture the corner of the park filled with refreshment stands catering for its youthful visitors: gingerbread stalls, purveyors of curds and whey, and half a dozen cows providing fresh milk – precursors of the 'freshly squeezed' drinks available today.

Walk up the steps to Carlton House Terrace (built by Nash, 1827–32), presided over by the statue of the 'Grand Old Duke of York' (Prince Frederick, Duke of York and Albany, 1763–1827, brother of George IV). The Duke surmounts what one contemporary critic described as 'a bad imitation of Trajan's Column, very mean and poor in appearance'. Note the modestly sized wooden door in the column's base, facing the park. For sixpence, you might ascend the narrow spiral staircase inside the column, consisting of 168 steps, to obtain a panoramic view of the West End. Such viewings were, however, limited to '12 to 4pm, from May to Sept. 24th, during which period alone the atmosphere of London is clear enough to allow the view to be seen'.

From Carlton House Terrace, walk down Waterloo Place. You are approaching Pall Mall – the heart of 'Clubland'. Nineteenth-century gentlemen's clubs had particular criteria for membership: some were party political; others had different requirements. The Travellers' Club (106 Pall Mall, built 1832), for example, catered for foreigners and diplomats, stipulating that members 'must have

A typical Clubland interior, photographed in the 1890s.

Dickens' club, the Athenaeum, Waterloo Place (built 1829–30).

travelled at least 500 miles from London'. All boasted sumptuous facilities: libraries, smoking rooms, dining rooms, overnight accommodation, in a style fit for an English gentleman.

Before you turn left on to Pall Mall, you will pass Dickens' own club, the Athenaeum. Built in 1829–30 in the Greek style, the club has an extravagant frieze, copied from the Panathenaic procession of the Parthenon, and a golden Pallas Athene atop the entrance. To set foot inside its marbled halls, a man had to be known for scientific, literary or artistic attainment, and membership was, therefore, a badge of honour (although 'noblemen and gentlemen distinguished as liberal patrons of science, literature, and the arts' were also eligible). Despite this, it seems Dickens was not entirely comfortable in Clubland and reportedly 'seldom spoke to anyone unless previously addressed'. His only mention of a 'clubbable' character in his novels is the not very sympathetic Mr Twemlow in *Our Mutual Friend*, who goes to his club, 'promptly secures a large window, writing materials, and all the newspapers, and establishes himself; immoveable, to be respectfully contemplated by Pall Mall'.

Pall Mall itself, it might be argued, presents the Victorian ideal of a public thoroughfare: wide and flanked by impressive classical architecture. Certainly, grand carriages of the upper classes, phaetons and landaus, bearing a family crest, would trundle along its broad expanse, whether to levees at St James's Palace or simply dropping silk-suited gentlemen at the portico of their club. In 1807, Pall Mall became the first street in London to be lit by gas, attested by a plaque at No. 100, and several buildings still possess distinctive vintage gaslights. It was a thoroughly respectable street – and hence it becomes the home of conman Montague Tigg in *Martin Chuzzlewit*, as he affects the trappings of gentility.

There is a marvellous counterpoint to the grandeur of Pall Mall, as one turns right into St James's Street: one of the few London alleys that still leads to a Dickensian 'court' (an enclosed courtyard of houses or tenements). Beside the wine merchants Berry Bros & Rudd (who have been situated on St James's Street since 1698) lies Pickering Place. A plaque here marks a peculiar piece of history – it was home to the legation of the briefly independent Republic of Texas in the 1840s – and the courtyard contains a bust of Lord Palmerston (Prime Minister 1855–8 and 1859–65), who also resided in the vicinity. Despite such impressive inhabitants, the secluded yard had a mixed reputation: it was home to several notorious 'gaming-houses' in the 1830s and 1840s, beloved by the more louche members of the upper classes.

Continue down St James's Street and you will notice Lock & Co ('Ladies and Gentlemen's Caps and Hats', founded in 1676), which retains a typically Georgian shop front. A little further along, turn

An impressive old gaslight on Pall Mall.

A late-Victorian photograph of Pall Mall and Waterloo Place.

Above: Pickering Place, a hidden courtyard off St James's Street.

Below left: Lock & Co, hatters, St James's Street (founded 1676).

Below right: Paxton & Whitfield, cheesemongers, Jermyn Street.

right down Jermyn Street, to compare Lock & Co with the more grandiose nineteenth-century exterior of Paxton & Whitfield, cheesemongers to Queen Victoria. You are now looking at a shop front that was 'modern' in the Victorian period: large plate-glass windows, stucco decoration, gilding, a window that would have been lit nightly with countless jets of gas. Both these shops are rare survivals. The loss of such establishments, especially purveyors of food, is one of the most significant changes between the past and present. A street directory from the 1850s, for example, shows that Jermyn Street – although a thoroughly aristocratic area – still boasted a grocer, fruiterer, three butchers, two cheesemongers, a baker and a fishmonger.

Opposite the cheesemonger's is St James's Church. Step inside and you will find a beautiful interior, designed by Christopher Wren, consecrated in 1684, but damaged in the Blitz and later restored. The reredos and organ case, carved by Grinling Gibbons, are some of the sculptor's best work. The church is the setting for the wedding of the scheming Mr Lammle in *Our Mutual Friend*, resident of nearby Sackville Street.

Walk through the church and you will find yourself in Piccadilly (see *Opening Hours and Alternative Routes* above, if closed). Opposite you once stood a row of imposing aristocratic mansions, most of which have long since vanished. There are, however, two notable

The interior of St James's Church, Piccadilly (consecrated 1684).

survivals. Cross the road, turn left, and, after you have passed Sackville Street, you will see the Albany, an odd courtyard rather hidden from the main road. This was originally a private residence for the first Viscount Melbourne, converted into 'bachelor chambers' in 1802. Inhabited by many famous Victorians (including Palmerston, Gladstone and Bulwer-Lytton), this peculiar aristocratic close is also home to *Our Mutual Friend's* supercilious Fledgeby, who covertly profits as a moneylender in the City. After the Albany comes the other old property, Burlington House, now the home of the Royal Academy. The building dates back to 1664–5, although much enlarged and altered. It was acquired in 1854 by the government, who used it to house various learned societies.

The exterior of the Royal Academy (1860s).

Leave Piccadilly by turning right, through the Burlington Arcade, a Regency creation (1819). Its façade was altered in the twentieth century but the interior retains its original features, and one can also spot that rare survival, the 'Burlington Arcade beadle', a top-hatted security guard, retained by the Arcade's management to maintain decency and order. Originally the beadles of the Arcade wore a

Christmas lights in the Burlington Arcade, Piccadilly (built 1819).

Late-Victorian photograph of the Burlington Arcade, Piccadilly.

more ornate costume and sat in easy chairs by the entrances, 'to strike awe into the souls of vagrant boys'. They did little, however, to keep out the superior class of West End prostitute, for whom the Arcade was a notorious haunt. The higher class of London demi-mondaine bribed the beadles to let them walk here unmolested. It is not hard to populate this precinct in your mind – to picture crinolined ladies of fashionable dress and dubious character attempting to catch the eye of 'flash' young men.

The northern entrance of the Arcade brings you to Burlington Gardens and old Mayfair. Turn right and notice the bow-windowed No. 8, which contains one of the London branches of Ede & Ravenscroft (London's oldest tailors, established in 1689). To the left is Savile Row, internationally famous for fine tailoring. This district was, however, still largely residential in Dickens' period, and handsome Georgian and Victorian town-houses that would have belonged to Mayfair's elite can still be seen. Number 17 Savile Row is an interesting example where a plain Georgian front has been given a distinctly Victorian ironwork balcony and additional stucco. Note, too, the oversized gaslights on the gateposts and the link-snuffers below – taking us back to a period when link-boys carried flaming torches to illuminate one's way home through the London fog, for the price of a penny.

Walk down Savile Row until it becomes Mill Street, and follow the road to the left. You will find yourself next to St George's, Hanover Square. Built in the 1720s, to suit the fashionable district that had grown up in Mayfair, it was the first church in London with a portico. The church is somewhat hidden by the surrounding buildings but was the most fashionable venue for a Mayfair wedding (Disraeli married here in 1839). Nicholas Nickleby's mother idly dreams of a wedding at St George's for her daughter Kate – unfortunately with the cad Sir Mulberry Hawk as the bridegroom.

Distinctive gaslights and 'link-snuffers' at 17 Savile Row, Mayfair.

Kate Nickleby is insulted by the aristocratic Mulberry Hawk in *Nicholas Nickleby*.

Head northwards, through Hanover Square itself. Built up from 1717 into the 1720s, the area has lost much of its Georgian splendour. The town-houses at Nos. 20 and 24 are the only surviving (now listed) original buildings. Dickens' sister Fanny was a pupil and boarder at the prestigious Royal Academy of Music, not far from here, in Tenterden Street. Her father's penury put a premature end to Fanny's musical training. At the junction with Hanover Street stood the Hanover Square Rooms, a public meeting hall. Dickens appeared there on several occasions, performing amateur theatricals and giving public readings of his works.

On the far side of the square, walk down Harewood Place and cross busy Oxford Street, then continue straight ahead down Holles Street to Cavendish Square.

At first, it is hard to believe this is Dickens territory at all. The department stores of Oxford Street encroach on the southern side; an underground car park renders the central ornamental gardens a glorified roundabout. Chandos Street, at the north-eastern corner, retains a little more of the original feel of the district – not least Chandos House at the far end of the road (currently the headquarters of the Royal Society of Medicine; built as a property speculation in 1769).

Cavendish Square is where Madame Mantalini exploits poor Kate Nickleby in her exclusive dressmaker's shop. It is within a short distance of the Harley Street home of the unscrupulous banker Merdle, in *Little Dorrit*. It is on the corner of this square that scheming Silas Wegg pitches his shoddy wares, and later returns in splendour, as companion of the dust-heap owner Mr Boffin, in *Our Mutual Friend*. The miserable home of Mr Dombey – who knows the price of everything and the value of nothing – is also somewhere in this district. This conflux of plots and characters is not coincidental. If you feel a little envious of the beautiful town-houses of Mayfair and St James's, the works of the great author may offer you some meagre consolation. Consider all the Dickens characters just mentioned. They have one thing in common: they are all made miserable or corrupted by the pursuit of money.

From Chandos House, continue westwards along Queen Anne Street to its termination at Welbeck Street (where you may notice a plaque to Sir Patrick Manson, 'Father of modern tropical medicine'). Turn left, then immediately right along Bentinck Street (one of the many places in London in which Dickens' father took lodgings for his family), and you will come to Manchester Square.

This square is the end of our tour. It is a location which also gives you a rare chance to explore the interior of a West End mansion. Left to the nation in 1897, the Wallace Collection of art and

First-floor drawing room at the Wallace Collection.

antiquities sits in a house that was formerly the property of the Marquesses of Hertford. The building was extensively remodelled by Richard Wallace, illegitimate son of the fourth Marquess, to house the family's growing number of artworks; but it will give you an idea of the size and scale of such homes. The curved driveway — wide enough for a hansom cab or a carriage — still survives, as does a fine portico. It was here that nineteenth-century guests of the Marquess's family would alight; and it is here that we must leave the reader.

FOCUS ON: *PICCADILLY*

Piccadilly was one of the great avenues of Victorian London, lined on its northern side with grand mansions — 'the nearest approach to the Parisian boulevard of which London can boast'. It was also home to the great and the good. The Duke of Wellington lived in Apsley House at Hyde Park Corner until his death in 1852. Various members of the Rothschild dynasty established themselves in the western portion of the road, opposite Green Park (a highly respectable area, not least because of its proximity to Buckingham Palace). They included Walter Rothschild, an ardent animal lover and obsessive collector of zoological specimens, who drove a carriage pulled by six zebras around London, to prove his belief that the animals could be tamed.

The street itself went through various phases in a typical day. An early-morning pedestrian would have seen a procession of carts coming from the market gardens in the west of the metropolis, heading for Covent Garden market. Workmen might stop to take a sip of coffee from one of several open-air coffee stalls by the park. Clerks and office workers would appear next, an hour or two after the labourer, no doubt casting an admiring glance at the shop girls performing the daily rite of dressing shop windows.

During the afternoon Piccadilly was a fashionable place to stroll and be seen, not least in the Burlington Arcade. The Arcade's social exclusivity had waned a little by 1900, when 'young bloods from Tufnell Park and Acton and Tooting Bec' (middle-class suburbs) made a point of congregating there after work. Dressed in 'frock coats, highly polished hats and lavender gloves', these young men posed in groups, leaning on gold- and silver-mounted walking sticks, hoping to

A fashionable West End gentleman, from the 1840s.

'give the impression to passers-by that they are all heirs to peerages and great estates and are just out for an airing'. During the London 'season' (when the upper classes assembled in the capital for the annual summer round of social engagements and events) finely dressed 'swells' might also saunter into the Royal Academy, whose exhibition of art, between May and July, could make or break a budding painter.

Piccadilly also had two entertainment venues that drew visitors by day and by night (both demolished in 1905). The first was the Egyptian Hall, a building opened in 1812 whose unique selling point was a façade in the style of a Pharaoh's tomb. It hosted 'popular entertainments, lectures, and exhibitions', which included anything from the appearance of Tom Thumb in 1844, promoted by Phineas T. Barnum, to the popular magic shows of Maskelyne and Cooke, who were so successful that they had a residency in the building from 1873 to 1904. The second venue was St James's Hall, a magnificent 2,500-seat concert hall, brilliantly lit by a host of 'gas stars of seven jets each, suspended from the ceiling'. By the 1880s the hall's excellent acoustics had turned it into London's principal concert venue. Musicians such as Grieg, Liszt and Tchaikovsky gave concerts there. Dickens himself used the hall to perform and act out readings from his novels in the 1860s.

These readings, together with associated touring and promotion, were immensely lucrative but left the great man physically and emotionally exhausted – in particular, his rendition of the murder of Nancy in *Oliver Twist*. George Dolby, Dickens' stage manager, wrote of the effect these performances had on the reader and the audience:

The terrible force with which the actual perpetration of this most foul murder was described was of such a kind as to render Mr Dickens utterly prostrate for some moments after its delivery; and it was not until he had vanished from the platform that the public had sufficiently recovered their composure to appreciate the circumstance that the horrors to which they had been listening were but a story and not a reality.

Many believe that Dickens' readings contributed to his declining health and, ultimately, his death.

Dickens giving a reading in 1859.

THE HOUSES OF HARLEY STREET
From *Little Dorrit*

Upon that establishment of state, the Merdle establishment in Harley Street, Cavendish Square, there was the shadow of no more common wall than the fronts of other establishments of state on the opposite side of the street. Like unexceptionable Society, the opposing rows of houses in Harley Street were very grim with one another. Indeed, the mansions and their inhabitants were so much alike in that respect, that the people were often to be found drawn up on opposite sides of dinner-tables, in the shade of their own loftiness, staring at the other side of the way with the dullness of the houses.

Everybody knows how like the street the two dinner-rows of people who take their stand by the street will be. The expressionless uniform twenty houses, all to be knocked at and rung at in the same form, all approachable by the same dull steps, all fended off by the same pattern of railing, all with the same impracticable fire-escapes, the same inconvenient fixtures in their heads, and everything without exception to be taken at a high valuation — who has not dined with these? The house so drearily out of repair, the occasional bow-window, the stuccoed house, the newly-fronted house, the corner house with nothing but angular rooms, the house with the blinds always down, the house with the hatchment always up, the house where the collector has called for one quarter of an Idea, and found nobody at home — who has not dined with these? The house that nobody will take, and is to be had a bargain — who does not know her? The showy house that was taken for life by the disappointed gentleman, and which does not suit him at all — who is unacquainted with that haunted habitation?

Harley Street, Cavendish Square, was more than aware of Mr and Mrs Merdle. Intruders there were in Harley Street, of whom it was not aware; but Mr and Mrs Merdle it delighted to honour. Society was aware of Mr and Mrs Merdle. Society had said 'Let us license them; let us know them.'

Mr Merdle was immensely rich; a man of prodigious enterprise; a Midas without the ears, who turned all he touched to gold. He was in everything good, from banking to building. He was in Parliament, of course. He was in the City, necessarily. He was Chairman of this, Trustee of that, President of the other. The weightiest of men had said to projectors, 'Now, what name have you got? Have you got Merdle?' And, the reply being in the negative, had said, 'Then I won't look at you.'

WALK 2:
SOHO AND COVENT GARDEN

Starting location: Haymarket, SW1Y 4HT.

Nearest tube station: Piccadilly Circus.

Walking time: 1¼ to 1½ hours.

Opening hours and alternative routes:

- ST GILES-IN-THE-FIELDS CHURCH: daily, 9 a.m. to 6 p.m. *If the church and churchyard are closed, turn right at the Resurrection Gate, go down the alley, then turn left on to Stacey Street, left again on to New Compton Street, and right on to St Giles's Passage, leading to Mercer Street on the opposite side of Shaftesbury Avenue.*

- LONDON TRANSPORT MUSEUM: Monday to Thursday and Saturday to Sunday, 10 a.m. to 6 p.m. (last admission 5.15 p.m.); Friday, 11 a.m. to 6 p.m. (last admission 5.15 p.m.).

THE MODERN HAYMARKET is an integral part of London's 'Theatreland', with the Haymarket Theatre (completed in 1821, designed by Nash) and Her Majesty's Theatre (1897) dominating either side of the avenue. Each have had several previous incarnations, stretching back to the early eighteenth century. In Dickens' time, Her Majesty's, also known as Her Majesty's Opera House, was the leading location for opera: the great soprano Jenny Lind made her London debut there in 1847; *Fidelio* was premiered there in 1851. Meanwhile, at the Haymarket Theatre, most of the leading actors and actresses of the Victorian age,

The Haymarket Theatre (built 1821).

WALK 2

including Madame Vestris, Samuel Phelps and Mr and Mrs Charles Kean, appeared on stage.

Dickens himself had a lifelong passion for the theatre, having flirted with entering the acting profession as a young man. His enthusiasm for staging amateur productions was legendary. Among other theatrical ventures, he took the play *The Frozen Deep*, written by Wilkie Collins originally as an amusement for Dickens and his friends, to the Manchester Free Trade Hall in 1857. The purpose was charitable – to give benefit performances for the widow of the humourist Douglas Jerrold – but Dickens tackled the production with his usual method and rigour. It was for these highly successful Manchester shows that a young professional actress was hired – Ellen Ternan, the woman who would become Dickens' mistress. Miss Ternan went on to work for two years in London at the Haymarket Theatre.

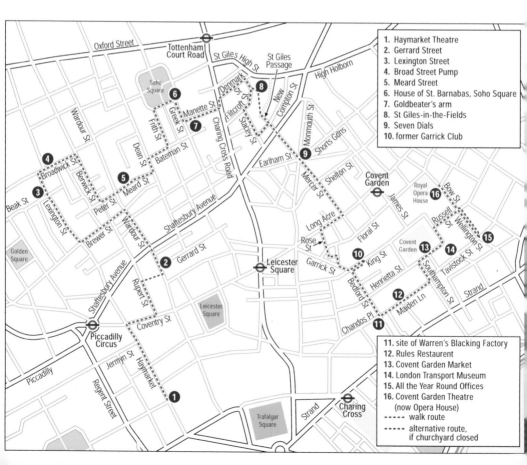

1. Haymarket Theatre
2. Gerrard Street
3. Lexington Street
4. Broad Street Pump
5. Meard Street
6. House of St. Barnabas, Soho Square
7. Goldbeater's arm
8. St Giles-in-the-Fields
9. Seven Dials
10. former Garrick Club

11. site of Warren's Blacking Factory
12. Rules Restaurent
13. Covent Garden Market
14. London Transport Museum
15. All the Year Round Offices
16. Covent Garden Theatre
(now Opera House)
----- walk route
····· alternative route,
if churchyard closed

The theatre's exterior is unchanged, and it is easy to stand below the grand portico and imagine Victorian theatre-goers milling about the pavement in a sea of tall hats and crinolines. Did Dickens mingle with the crowds, then slip backstage to see the young woman with whom he was besotted? The novelist's adultery was, of course, a well-kept secret. The pavements outside the theatre, on the other hand, contained a much more blatant affront to Victorian morality. Begin your walk northwards to the top of the street (where a modern gift shop occupies an original bow-windowed Georgian façade) and imagine it is nightfall. The road is lit by yellow, shimmering gas. The nearby streets, between the Haymarket and Leicester Square, contain numerous late-night coffee houses, refreshment rooms, drinking dens and dance halls. Constantly moving between them are groups of unaccompanied women. These are the Haymarket's 'demi-mondaines', or prostitutes: for this street was once synonymous with vice. No respectable woman would walk in the Haymarket after dark; and every man could expect to be

An 1857 sketch of Haymarket prostitutes, published in *Punch*.

A solitary Georgian shop front on the Haymarket.

importuned. As one letter-writer put it in 1846: 'Whether you are young and handsome, or old and ugly, will matter not; you will, in either case, be received with terms of endearment.' It is perhaps fitting that we begin with Dickens' affair and the 'fallen women' of the West End; for this will be something of a 'low' tour, through back streets and nineteenth-century slums.

Turn right on to Coventry Street. We shall skirt around Leicester Square, which in the Victorian era hosted a range of entertainments, including rifle galleries (such as that of Mr George in *Bleak House*), a music hall, dioramas, freak shows and a more sedate but long-lived attraction, 'Miss Linwood's Exhibition of Needlework' (which Peggotty visits in *David Copperfield*: 'a Mausoleum of needlework, favourable to self-examination and repentance'). Instead, turn left up Rupert Street, and watch for the Blue Posts public house on the right. Walk through the unusual double-storey archway beside it. At the end of the paved alleyway turn left on to Wardour Street and enter the heart of Soho.

In the eighteenth century this district housed aristocratic families in Golden Square (which becomes the somewhat decrepit home of Ralph Nickleby in *Nicholas Nickleby*) and Soho Square; but its social standing was in decline by the nineteenth century, its ancient, narrow streets increasingly home to immigrants from France, Germany and Italy. Houses were subdivided into rented rooms, ground floors turned into shop fronts or workshops. The upper classes moved away westwards, a process accentuated by a cholera epidemic in the 1850s. Yet, ironically, it was this decline that set the pattern for Soho's commercial future. Some of these foreigners opened small continental-style café-restaurants, a novelty in London, establishing an eclectic mix of cuisines and dining in the heart of the city.

The same effect was repeated with the Chinese community moving into 'Chinatown' in the 1950s. Gerrard Street, on your right, is the most visible example of the Chinese presence, with even its street signs translated into Chinese script. Dickens knew this road well. It was here that his uncle, Thomas Culliford Barrow, lodged in the 1820s, incapacitated by a compound fracture of his leg. The ten-year-old Dickens often visited his uncle and became, as he wrote in later years, 'your little companion and nurse, through a weary illness'. (Barrow's leg eventually had to be amputated and critics have correlated this with the large number of amputees and wooden legs in Dickens' fiction.) Almost forty years later, Dickens placed the gloomy house of the lawyer Mr Jaggers on Gerrard Street. It is described in *Great Expectations* as 'a stately house of its kind, but dolefully in want of painting, and with dirty windows', whose 'carved garlands on the panelled walls' remind Pip of a hangman's noose.

Continue north along Wardour Street, crossing Shaftesbury Avenue (a new street built in the 1880s), and turn left on to Brewer Street. Then take a right, down Lexington Street. At the junction with Beak Street, modern buildings yield to Georgian houses. They are now virtually all shops and cafés at street level. However, a glance at an 1850s street directory soon reveals the Victorian residents of Soho: we have only to replace the modern art gallery with the aptly named 'William Mash, Potato Dealer', the fashionable delicatessen with 'George Batten, Chesemonger'. The actual premises in question are a remarkable constant, exactly the sort of small shop – the converted ground floor of a Georgian house – with which Dickens himself would have been familiar. It is also in this area, a short distance from Golden Square, that Newman Noggs, the kindly clerk of *Nicholas Nickleby,* has his abode, and, among Soho's back alleys, that Little Emily, the troubled 'fallen woman' of *David Copperfield*, is discovered in 'low lodgings' of the worst calibre.

Now turn right from Lexington Street on to Broadwick Street. The public house on the corner is named after John Snow, the doctor

A Georgian shop front (with modern glazing) in Lexington Street, Soho.

The model of the Soho pump, commemorating Dr John Snow's investigations into water-borne cholera.

who plotted the progress of the Soho cholera outbreak of the 1850s and showed that the disease was transmitted in the local water supply, drawn from a pump on Broad Street (now Broadwick Street). Snow's findings were a revelation, when most people believed that 'miasma' (foul-smelling air) was the transmission method for all contagious disease. Sadly, they were not widely accepted until after his death in 1858. A posthumous tribute to Snow, a replica of the Broad Street pump, can be found on the left-hand side of the road.

Follow Broadwick Street to the junction with Berwick Street and turn right. This road retains a typical Soho mix of sex shops (a staple of the district since the 1960s), fashionable cafés and boutiques, and a thriving fruit and vegetable market (the only traditional street market in the West End, dating back to the eighteenth century). Turn left on to Peter Street, and cross Wardour Street. We have followed a rather circuitous route to come back to Meard Street, whose houses, with their tall sashes and stucco-clad lintels, built between 1722 and 1732, still give a flavour of the

Georgian homes in Meard Street, Soho, built in the 1720s.

residential side of old Soho. From Meard Street, turn left on to Dean Street, right on to Bateman Street, and left on to Frith Street, which also contains similar period properties.

Do not be fooled, as you approach Soho Square, by the black and white timbered gardener's hut at the centre, an early-twentieth-century 'Tudorbethan' creation. Instead, walk to the corner of Greek Street. The large house that dominates the eastern street corner is the House of St Barnabas.

Inside the House of St Barnabas, Soho Square.

Between 1811 and 1862 it housed the Westminster Commissioner for Works for Sewers, and then the Metropolitan Board of Works. It was here, therefore, that initial plans for Joseph Bazalgette's grand sewer networks were drawn up – a crucial development in London's infrastructure, constructed 1858–65. Since 1862 the property has been owned by the House of Charity. This charitable body originally provided a shelter for 'respectable persons who are plunged into misfortune', but now focuses on training and educational opportunities for the homeless. The garden at the rear contains a remarkable Romanesque chapel (built 1862–4) and is widely believed to be the inspiration for Dr Manette's garden in *A Tale of Two Cities*. We leave Soho along Manette Street, running alongside the house's perimeter, beside the Pillars of Hercules pub; the street was renamed after the Dickens character in 1895.

The garden of 'Dr Manette's house' in Soho.

At the end of Manette Street is Charing Cross Road (another new road of the 1880s, built through some of the worst central slums). Cross over, turn left and then right down Denmark Street, with its array of music shops. At the end of the street is the historic church of St Giles-in-the-Fields, a building whose foundation can be traced back to a twelfth-century leper hospital.

WALK 2

A replica of the goldbeater's sign mentioned in *A Tale of Two Cities* can be seen on Manette Street.

The Resurrection Gate at St Giles-in-the-Fields (built 1800).

The present church dates from 1733 and is little changed from Dickens' day. A peculiar hidden feature is the 'Resurrection Gate' (built 1800, containing a copy of a bas-relief of the Resurrection first carved in 1687) on the church's western side. It was moved to its current location from the northern entrance in 1865, possibly in anticipation of the construction of Charing Cross Road. Unfortunately, the new boulevard was built on a route that bypassed the church entirely, condemning this distinctive grand entrance to open on to the dingy back alley of Flitcroft Street.

Walk through the church (you may need to use the entrance on St Giles High Street) and admire its beautiful interior, then leave from the southern entrance via the gate that leads down St Giles Passage. Walking straight ahead will lead you across New Compton Street, then across Shaftesbury Avenue, to Mercer Street. This road terminates in one of London's most unusual traffic roundabouts – the Victorians would have called it a 'circus' – the junction of seven narrow roads, Seven Dials. It is now a fashionable shopping district but it used to be the centre of one of the worst, most dangerous slums in the Victorian metropolis.

The Doric column at the centre of this peculiar roundabout gave the district its name, bearing six sundials at its pinnacle (it is said that the column itself provides the seventh dial). The current monument, however, is a modern replica of the original that stood from 1694 to 1773. Dickens was very familiar with the Dials, if not the obelisk. In *Sketches by Boz* he describes two drunken women fighting here ('Vy don't you pitch into her, Sarah?' ... 'I'd tear her precious eyes out – a wixen!'); he mentions the 'ill-proportioned and deformed ... half-naked children' to be found in the gutters, and the second-hand clothes stalls of Monmouth Street. The area was a byword for slum life, its shoddy tenements filled with the poorest of the poor; there was no decent sanitation; rooms were divided and

The interior of St Giles-in-the-Fields (built 1733).

subdivided; families lived in cellars together with pigs and donkeys, and windows were smashed, or 'glazed' with brown paper. Many of its inhabitants were Irish, trying to escape poverty and famine in their homeland. It was a district into which middle-class Victorians would not venture in darkness, without the aid of a police officer. Dickens himself undertook such a perilous journey in his journalistic piece 'On Duty with Inspector Field' (1851), accompanying the police on a nocturnal visit to the 'Rats' Castle', a thieves' den in the heart of the slum. In his fiction, however, Seven Dials makes only one notable appearance: when Nicholas and Kate Nickleby become lost and stumble upon the rakish Mr Mantalini – reduced to turning a mangle for his new partner in life, a vituperative washerwoman.

Find Mercer Street on the far side of the Dials monument, follow it downhill, cross Shelton Street and carry on all the

A slum street in Seven Dials.

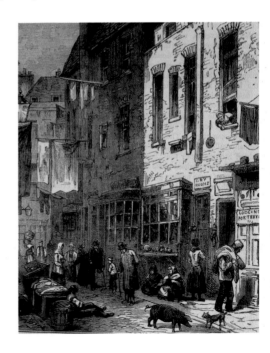

way down to Long Acre. In the nineteenth century Long Acre was the district for carriage makers, but there is little evidence of that trade nowadays. Turn right, and you will find Stanford's map shop on the opposite side of the road; it has an excellent historical section, should you wish to explore the Victorian metropolis further. Then turn left down Rose Street, a narrow alley, by the side of the shop, and cross Floral Street. Rose Street continues its winding course, taking you past the Lamb and Flag pub (established 1623). Take a left on to Garrick Street.

The street is named after the eighteenth-century actor David Garrick and it was part of Dickens' affinity with the theatre that he was a member of the Garrick Club, whose original purpose was to provide a place where 'actors and men of refinement and education might meet on equal terms'. Turn left on to King Street and you will pass the original location of the club at No. 35 (it has resided at 15 Garrick Street since 1864). It was in 1858 at the old King Street club-house that Dickens and another literary giant, William Makepeace Thackeray, engaged in a battle over the club membership of Edmund Yates. Yates, a journalist protégé of Dickens, had written a highly unflattering article about Thackeray; and an increasing enmity between the two men was fuelled by Thackeray's disapproval of Dickens' public (and rather cruel) separation from his wife, Catherine. Dickens, in turn, suspected Thackeray of spreading gossip (albeit truthful) about himself and 'an actress'. The result was that Yates was expelled from the club and Dickens resigned.

The author William Makepeace Thackeray, Dickens' contemporary.

Thackeray and Dickens would not speak again until a chance meeting at the Athenaeum Club in 1863, shortly before Thackeray's death.

Covent Garden market lies ahead but, for the moment, turn around, and take a left turn down Bedford Street, passing the entrance to St Paul's Church. You will come to a junction where Chandos Place is on your right and the narrow entry to Maiden Lane on your left. This corner of Chandos Place was the second location at which Dickens worked, aged twelve, for Warren's blacking factory. It was onerous manual labour (pasting and labelling pots of boot-black), which he found deeply humiliating and degrading – not least because he could be seen by passers-by through the shop window.

Now turn down Maiden Lane. This street contains a famous London institution, Rules Restaurant, which began life as an oyster shop in 1798. Dickens dined there, as did most of the elite of Victorian London, the future Edward VII using it as a discreet venue to dine with his mistress.

At the end of Maiden Lane, turn left up Southampton Street. We come at last to Covent Garden market. Now devoted exclusively to shopping, it was the principal wholesale market for fruit, vegetables and flowers in the West End until 1974. It has not changed much in the last 180 years. The piazza was laid out by Inigo Jones in 1631 and the neo-classical central buildings date from 1828–30 (though not roofed over

Dickens at the blacking factory; an illustration by Frederick Barnard.

until 1872). In the nineteenth century, it would have been filled not with tourists but with carts unloading goods, costers haggling over stock for their barrows, and 'two-bunches-a-penny' flower-girls filling their baskets with cheap violets and sweet-peas.

Rules Restaurant, Maiden Lane, Covent Garden.

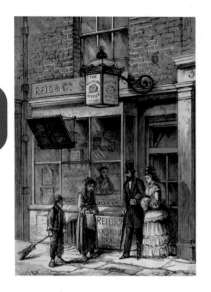

Rules Restaurant began as an oyster shop, like this one in Drury Lane, in 1798.

Dickens became familiar with the market as a boy, while working at Warren's, and it appears in much of his fiction. Tom Pinch wanders around the market in *Martin Chuzzlewit*; Steerforth stays in a hotel in the piazza in *David Copperfield*, where David treats him to dessert and wine; David buys Dora flowers here and takes lodgings nearby. Arthur Clenham of *Little Dorrit* likewise has accommodation in Covent Garden; Pip of *Great Expectations* joins a gentlemen's drinking club that dines at a Covent Garden hotel and, later, also finds a hotel room. Indeed, Dickens' default location for slightly lost young men looking for lodgings always seems the same. This is, perhaps, not unrelated to the slightly louche, nocturnal world of 'supper and song clubs' and hotels that surrounded the market precincts.

The best Victorian 'experience' in Covent Garden may be the London Transport Museum, housed in old market buildings in the south-eastern corner of the piazza. It contains, among other things, a horse-drawn omnibus (first seen in London in 1829), which visitors can sit inside. You might, however, wish to save it for the end of your walk. So first leave the piazza by Russell Street on the eastern side.

The Transport Museum's horse-drawn omnibus takes a rare excursion on a modern street.

Turn right down Wellington Street and you will see the Dickens Coffee House. It deserves the name because Dickens edited his magazine *All the Year Round* in the offices above and had a suite of private apartments here – a blue plaque testifies to the location.

Double back up Wellington Street. On the right, after Russell Street, is the now defunct Bow Street Magistrates' Court (Bow Street appears in *Oliver Twist*; but this later version was built in 1879–81). On the left is the Royal Opera House, designed by E. M. Barry in 1858. Dickens would doubtless have

A letter by Dickens, written on *All the Year Round* office notepaper.

observed the theatre's construction. He must also have occasionally thought back to 1832, when, aged twenty, he applied to the manager of the Covent Garden Theatre, the Opera House's predecessor, asking for an audition. Dickens did not attend, owing to 'a terrible bad cold and an inflammation of the face'. His enthusiasm subsequently waned and he did not write to the theatre again – a fortunate chance, perhaps, for generations of readers.

The Floral Hall, originally built as a new market hall for Covent Garden (1858–9), now part of the Royal Opera House.

WALK 2

FOCUS ON: *COVENT GARDEN*

The great fruit and vegetable market of Covent Garden was situated in the heart of the Victorian capital. It was one of London's famous sights, and quite a respectable one: fashionable women might leave their carriages to seek out plants for their conservatories, or the finest fresh fruit; guidebooks directed visitors to admire Fowler's neo-classical arcade, filled with colourful produce ('A visit to this grand mart of vegetable produce cannot fail to gratify'). The market operated, however, on a very different schedule from its modern-day descendant.

Business began during the small hours of the night, as wagons and carts filled the surrounding streets, bringing traffic to a standstill. The wagons were all piled high; and great mounds of cabbages, cauliflowers and turnips could be built up to 12 feet or so with a 'wall-like regularity'. In the early nineteenth century the suppliers were farmers from the Home Counties, market gardeners from the outer suburbs of the metropolis, or the 'cockney nurserymen' living on the borders of the city. This changed with the coming of the railways, which could bring produce from much further afield, even the Continent. Hot-houses also made formerly seasonal fruits available for much of the year.

A woman worker carrying a basket of vegetables at Covent Garden.

The buyers arrived around dawn, which was the peak time for the market. Shopkeepers, often with their own carts, had regular arrangements with the sellers and took the finest specimens; but there was also a vast array of petty dealers with smaller carts, costermongers with barrows (two thousand donkey barrows might visit the market in a day), and even itinerant hawkers on foot, all of whom purchased their goods in the market precincts. The hawkers were expert in 'dressing' the oldest, mouldiest fruit and vegetables to make them appear acceptable to the buying public. The general noise and bustle was added to by the shouts of the sellers, not least the old street cry of 'All-a-growing all-a-blowing' that resounded around the square.

The market workers and hangers-on were themselves a sight: porters carrying tall columns of baskets; the van drivers, who had travelled throughout the night, taking a nap under their wagons; the Irishwomen who offered to carry goods home for you in 'half-humorous, half-pathetic tones'. There was also a legion of flower-girls, who purchased bunches of roses, violets, heathers and other flowers and then sat on the steps of St Paul's Church, subdividing the bunches into smaller ones, or buttonhole bouquets. The local spectacle was not, however, an entirely quaint one, and there was a dark side to the market's displays of abundance. Dickens, in his *Night Walks* (a famous piece of journalism from 1860), recalls 'children who prowl about this place; who sleep in the baskets, fight for the offal, dart at any object they think they can lay their thieving hands on, dive under the carts and barrows, dodge the constables, and are perpetually making a blunt pattering on the pavement of the Piazza with the rain of their naked feet'. One wonders if the ladies who visited the eastern galleries of the arcade to buy 'plants and flowers of a superior description' noticed the dirty, shoeless children, dodging the attention of the market beadle. James Greenwood, an 1860s journalist, writes a fascinating description of these same urchins: 'They will gather about a muck heap and gobble up plums, a sweltering mass of decay, and oranges and apples that have quite lost their original shape and colour, with the avidity of ducks or pigs' – a very Victorian image of plenty and poverty.

Haggling over produce at Covent Garden market.

WALK 2

THE MAZE OF SEVEN DIALS

From *Sketches by Boz*

The stranger who finds himself in 'The Dials' for the first time, and stands Belzoni-like, at the entrance of seven obscure passages, uncertain which to take, will see enough around him to keep his curiosity and attention awake for no inconsiderable time. From the irregular square into which he has plunged, the streets and courts dart in all directions, until they are lost in the unwholesome vapour which hangs over the house-tops, and renders the dirty perspective uncertain and confined; and lounging at every corner, as if they came there to take a few gasps of such fresh air as has found its way so far, but is too much exhausted already, to be enabled to force itself into the narrow alleys around, are groups of people, whose appearance and dwellings would fill any mind but a regular Londoner's with astonishment ... In addition to the numerous groups who are idling about the gin-shops and squabbling in the centre of the road, every post in the open space has its occupant, who leans against it for hours, with listless perseverance. It is odd enough that one class of men in London appear to have no enjoyment beyond leaning against posts. We never saw a regular bricklayer's labourer take any other recreation, fighting excepted. Pass through St Giles's in the evening of a week-day, there they are in their fustian dresses, spotted with brick-dust and whitewash, leaning against posts. Walk through Seven Dials on Sunday morning: there they are again, drab or light corduroy trousers, Blucher boots, blue coats, and great yellow waistcoats, leaning against posts. The idea of a man dressing himself in his best clothes, to lean against a post all day!

The peculiar character of these streets, and the close resemblance each one bears to its neighbour, by no means tends to decrease the bewilderment in which the unexperienced wayfarer through 'the Dials' finds himself involved. He traverses streets of dirty, straggling houses, with now and then an unexpected court composed of buildings as ill-proportioned and deformed as the half-naked children that wallow in the kennels. Here and there, a little dark chandler's shop, with a cracked bell hung up behind the door to announce the entrance of a customer, or betray the presence of some young gentleman in whom a passion for shop tills has developed itself at an early age: others, as if for support, against some handsome lofty building, which usurps the place of a low dingy public-house; long rows of broken and patched windows expose plants that may have flourished when 'the Dials' were built, in vessels as dirty as 'the Dials' themselves; and shops for the purchase of rags, bones, old iron, and kitchen-stuff, vie in cleanliness with the bird-fanciers and rabbit-dealers, which one might fancy so many arks, but for the irresistible conviction that no bird in its proper senses, who was permitted to leave one of them, would ever come back again. Brokers' shops, which would seem to have been established by humane individuals, as refuges for destitute bugs, interspersed with announcements of day-schools, penny theatres, petition-writers, mangles, and music for balls or routs, complete the 'still life' of the subject; and dirty men, filthy women, squalid children, fluttering shuttlecocks, noisy battledores, reeking pipes, bad fruit, more than doubtful oysters, attenuated cats, depressed dogs, and anatomical fowls, are its cheerful accompaniments.

WALK 3:
THE STRAND AND FLEET STREET

Tip: To get the most out of this walk, a weekday lunchtime will give you full access to the Temple and its gardens.

Starting location: Victoria Embankment, SW1A 2HE.

Nearest tube station: Embankment.

Walking time: 1 to 1¼ hours.

Opening hours and alternative routes:

- VICTORIA EMBANKMENT GARDENS: Monday to Saturday, 7.30 a.m. to dusk; Sunday, 9 a.m. to dusk. *If the gardens are shut, you can walk around them by going past the entrance to Embankment station, down Villiers Street (as if heading towards the Strand), then turning right into Watergate Walk.*

- THE TEMPLE: Monday to Friday, accessible during office hours (gardens accessible only from 12.30 p.m. to 3 p.m; Saturday and Sunday, access is limited to the Tudor Street gatehouse (see below), other gates are not open and the gardens are closed.

W E BEGIN OUR WALK just to the west of Hungerford Bridge. Built into the Embankment wall stands a monument to Joseph Bazalgette (1819–91), who was responsible for one of the greatest changes in the landscape of Dickens' London. We have already mentioned in passing the vast network of sewers that brought proper sanitation to much of the capital, under the aegis of the Metropolitan Board of Works, in the 1860s. This sculpture attests to Bazalgette's other, more visible triumph – the simultaneous creation of the Thames Embankment itself (the Latin inscription translates as 'He placed the river in chains'). Before the Embankment's construction, the Thames had a gradually sloping shore, abutted by rickety wharves and warehouses. It was here, for instance, that the Micawber family of *David Copperfield* 'lodged in a little, dirty, tumble-down public-house … whose protruding wooden rooms overhung the river', before their emigration.

Bazalgette's works, along the north bank of the Thames, replaced such buildings with a grand riverside avenue that was built not only for flood defence, but as a bypass for the crowded ancient route between Westminster and the City (the Strand/Fleet Street), as well as being a convenient structure to house his new sewers and a new underground railway line. Dickens watched Bazalgette's sewer scheme develop (a positive article appears in his magazine *All the Year Round* in 1861) but one wonders if he was quite in sympathy with the innovation. Certainly his last novels, *Our Mutual Friend* (1864–5) and *The Mystery of Edwin Drood* (1870), contain few hints of the momentous changes in London's topography during the 1860s.

Memorial to Joseph Bazalgette, creator of the Thames Embankment.

WALK 3

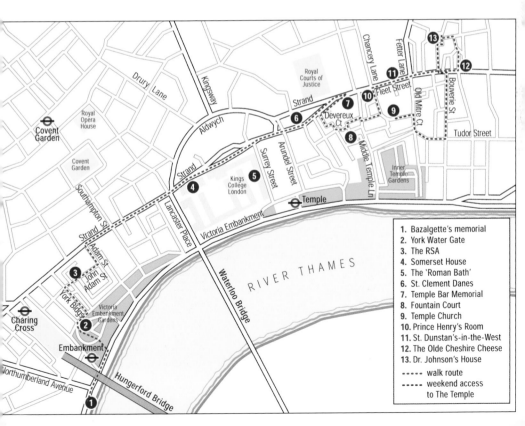

1. Bazalgette's memorial
2. York Water Gate
3. The RSA
4. Somerset House
5. The 'Roman Bath'
6. St. Clement Danes
7. Temple Bar Memorial
8. Fountain Court
9. Temple Church
10. Prince Henry's Room
11. St. Dunstan's-in-the-West
12. The Olde Cheshire Cheese
13. Dr. Johnson's House

----- walk route
----- weekend access to The Temple

Hungerford Market stood on the site of Charing Cross and Embankment stations from 1833 to 1854.

Cross over to Embankment station, and then walk into the adjoining Victoria Embankment Gardens. At the rear of the gardens, not far from the entrance, is a relic of the old riverside London that Bazalgette demolished. The 'York Water Gate' was built in 1626 – the earliest ornamental archway in London – as a decorative gateway to the Duke of Buckingham's York House. Note how the gate is in a sunken hollow in the gardens; this was once only a foot or two above the high-water mark of the Thames.

Exit the gardens by the gate to the right of the Water Gate, and glance down Buckingham Street. Dickens briefly lived in this area in 1834, while working as a journalist, on the cusp of his career as an author. He lived both in 15 Buckingham Street (demolished) and nearby Cecil Street (a road that no longer exists). Do not walk down Buckingham Street, but turn right and then go up the steps into York Buildings; Dickens also briefly found lodgings for his family here in the same year.

The York Water Gate.

The catacombs of the 'Adelphi Arches' redeveloped as an exhibition space within the Royal Society of Arts.

WALK 3

We are about to walk through the 'Adelphi', a district that appears repeatedly in Dickens' fiction, perhaps because he would often follow this very route from his riverside lodgings (David Copperfield, Dickens' fictionalised self, is also given lodgings in Buckingham Street and perambulates the district). The 3-acre site was originally an extensive neo-classical housing development, constructed by the Adam brothers in the 1770s. The brothers struggled to fund the project and, although the houses were of the best quality, the area never became truly fashionable. Beneath the houses lay a complex system of tunnels and vaults, to place the buildings on an elevation above the river. You can see the last public vestige of these tunnels in Lower Robert Street on the right, as you walk up York Buildings. In Dickens' time the vacant 'Adelphi arches' had become a notorious haunt for vagrants and criminals ('the chosen resort of thieves and bad characters of every kind').

Turn right up John Adam Street and walk its length. The Royal Society for the encouragement of Arts, Manufactures and Commerce (RSA), on the left, is part of the original Adelphi development. Founded in 1754, the Society awarded prizes to promote excellence in various fields of endeavour. It was the first body to hold a photographic exhibition in London, and also instigated the first scheme for marking historic houses with plaques. Dickens, involved in numerous literary and artistic organisations, was a member and served as vice-president.

Note also No. 7 Adam Street at the top of the road, which still has the Adam brothers' trademark façade. It is not far from here that Miss Wardle of *The Pickwick Papers* stops in Osborne's Hotel, and that Arthur Clenham spies on Tattycoram and Miss Wade in *Little Dorrit*.

Turn left down Adam Street, then right on to the Strand. You are standing on one of the great thoroughfares of the Victorian metropolis, but unfortunately there is little that survives from Dickens' time. On the north side of the road, you may notice Exchequer Court and several other narrow alleys, leading up to Maiden Lane in Covent Garden. These odd byways belong to Dickens' London, with gaslights that create an attractive effect after dark, but they are hardly very salubrious. The Savoy Hotel on the right dates to the 1880s. The grand

A typical Adelphi façade.

dining rooms of Simpson's in the Strand can trace their history back to the 'Grand Cigar Divan' that first opened in 1828; they are well worth a visit, but the current rooms date to a refit in 1904. Carry on down the Strand, therefore, until you come to the church of St Mary-le-Strand and, on your right, Somerset House.

The building was designed in 1775, although its east and west wings were added later, in the 1830s and 1850s respectively. The grand palatial courtyard and surrounding wings were intended to bring together several government departments under one roof, as well as various learned societies (the Royal Academy, the Royal Society and the Society of Antiquaries all had a home here during Dickens' youth). Significantly for our walk, this was also the building that housed the Royal Navy Pay Office – Dickens' father's employer – which recalled John Dickens to London in 1822 and hence brought Charles as a young boy to live in the city that would become his muse. The building is largely unchanged from the early nineteenth century; to see the interior, visit the Courtauld Art Gallery, which now occupies the north wing. It does not, however, appear in Dickens' fiction, barring a passing mention of a visit to the Legacy Duty Office in *The Pickwick Papers*.

Return to the Strand and turn right. St Mary-le-Strand (designed by James Gibbs, and built 1714–17) retains its ancient position in the middle of the road, but the buildings behind it were constructed during the creation of the Aldwych and Kingsway at the turn of the twentieth century (replacing Wych Street and Holywell Street, 'low' streets whose shops specialised in second-hand clothes and pornography respectively). Walk along the Strand past St Mary's. On the right you will see Surrey Street. If you walk down, you may see on the right a small sign that says 'Roman Bath: Down Steps Turn Right'. This London curiosity is mentioned in *David Copperfield*: 'There was an old Roman bath in those days at the bottom of one of the streets out of the Strand – it may be there still – in which I have had many a cold plunge.' There is some debate about its true antiquity, to say the least. Unfortunately, the bath is in a gated

The entrance to Somerset House.

Somerset House courtyard, looking west.

The Surrey Street 'Roman Bath' in the Victorian era.

alley, which is not always open, and the interior can be visited only by appointment with the National Trust.

Back on the Strand, continue towards St Clement Danes (built by Wren, 1679–82; steeple added by Gibbs in 1719–20). Now the church of the Royal Air Force, this is where the heroine of *Mrs Lirriper's Lodgings* was married and possesses 'a sitting in a very pleasant pew with genteel company and my own hassock'. Keep walking past the grand Gothic of the Royal Courts of Justice (planned shortly before Dickens' death but constructed in the 1870s) to the Temple Bar Memorial.

This is the spot where once stood Temple Bar, the ceremonial arched gateway that marked the western boundary of the City of London, the ancient mercantile heart of the capital. We will come to Temple Bar again – it has been re-erected further east – but the present monument, topped by a splendid griffin, occupies the arch's original location, before it was removed in 1878 to ease traffic congestion. Several of Dickens' characters pass through the old arch, including David Copperfield and Mr Dorrit, while Tellson's Bank in *A Tale of Two Cities* stands near to this spot.

Temple Bar takes its name from the hidden maze of courtyards, lanes and buildings that lie between Fleet Street and the river – the Middle Temple and Inner Temple, two of London's ancient 'Inns of Court'. These medieval colleges for legal practitioners (similar to the colleges of Oxford and Cambridge) came to occupy buildings and land that once belonged to the order of Knights Templar. The Inns survive to this day and comprise mainly Georgian and Victorian buildings, still used by members of the legal profession. They also still have a role in the education of barristers, who must belong to an Inn in order to be 'called to the bar'.

All the Inns (Middle Temple, Inner Temple, Lincoln's Inn, Gray's Inn) feature in Dickens' fiction, and he knew legal London well from his time as a law clerk (1827–9). The Temple area, therefore, will repay a visit. [*The following two paragraphs assume a weekday visit to the Temple. If you are visiting at the weekend, ignore the Temple for now and continue to Prince Henry's Room, opposite Chancery Lane.*]

There are several entrances and exits to the Temple along Fleet Street, but the easiest to find is perhaps Devereux Court, directly opposite the Royal Courts of Justice. So retrace your steps for 100 yards, turn into the narrow alley just before the George pub and enter the Temple at the gaslight-topped gate at the far end, on the left. You will soon find yourself in Fountain Court, where Westlock meets Ruth Pinch in *Martin Chuzzlewit*. Dickens writes in *Barnaby Rudge* of 'a clerkly monkish atmosphere, which public offices of law have not disturbed, and even legal firms have failed to scare away', and there is still something distinctly calming about the quiet seclusion of the Temple, despite its devotion to the cut and thrust of legal business.

Gaslights in Fountain Court, Temple.

Directly south of Fountain Court (straight on past the fountain) is Garden Court, where Pip and Herbert Pocket have chambers in *Great Expectations*. Mortimer Lightwood of *Our Mutual Friend* also lodges in the Temple. Turn left at the fountain, then cross Middle Temple Lane and go straight on; bearing left, you will come to the famous circular Temple Church (consecrated in 1185). You may wish to explore the gardens and grounds further (the gardens are open from 12.30 to 3 p.m.), but leave by Inner Temple Lane, to the left of the Temple Church.

You will find yourself back on Fleet Street next to a building that is half-timbered in its upper storeys – one of the few London dwellings that predate the Great Fire of 1666. Known as 'Prince Henry's Room', the principal room in the house contains evidence of its antiquity – a Jacobean

Above left: The Paschal Lamb, symbol of the Middle Temple, here atop a gaslight.

Above right: Pegasus, symbol of the Inner Temple, on a weathervane.

Left: 'Prince Henry's Room' on Fleet Street.

panelled ceiling and panelled walls – although its exact connection to Prince Henry, son of James I, is disputed. The house appears indirectly in *David Copperfield*, being the location of the 'perspiring wax work' to which David takes Peggotty. Mrs Salmon's Waxworks was a long-standing attraction that occupied the premises between 1795 and 1816. Its principal draw was a representation of the 'prophetess' Mother Shipton, an automaton that was 'an especial favourite with the juvenile visitors, as she used to put out her leg and kick the shins of anyone who approached her'.

Continue down Fleet Street past Chancery Lane. The church on the left is St Dunstan's-in-the-West. The current building dates to 1831 but the clock and accompanying bell-ringing giants (supposed by many to represent Gog and Magog, the traditional guardians of the City of London) are from 1671. The clock was erected to give thanks for the salvation of the church from the Great Fire of London and is reputedly the first in London to have had minutes marked on its dial. The church is famous in Victorian literature for its appearance in the 'penny dreadful' from which the Sweeney Todd myth arose ('The String of Pearls', published in 1846); but it also receives a passing mention in *David Copperfield* and *Barnaby Rudge*.

The clock of St Dunstan's-in-the-West, Fleet Street.

Our penultimate stop lies a little way further down Fleet Street, past Fetter Lane. Look for a series of narrow alleys leading from the north side of the road, and you will see Ye Olde Cheshire Cheese, one of London's oldest pubs, its unusual lamp and sign projecting into Wine Office Court. The well-preserved oak-beamed interior is a well-established tourist trap, but Dickens undoubtedly supped here and it may be the tavern to which Carton takes Darnay in *A Tale of Two Cities*.

Finally, continue along Wine Office Court away from the bustle of Fleet Street, bearing left to Gough Square. This is the site of Dr Johnson's House, with a museum dedicated to Samuel Johnson, the eighteenth-century man of letters, of *Dictionary* fame, but it is also a place of pilgrimage for Dickensians: it was to a building in Johnson's Court, which leads from Dr Johnson's House, that Dickens brought his first story for publication, to the offices of *The Monthly Magazine* (long since

The gaslight sign of Ye Olde Cheshire Cheese.

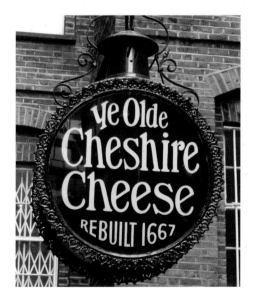

WALK 3

demolished). He describes how it was 'dropped stealthily one evening at twilight, with fear and trembling, into a dark letter-box, in a dark office, up a dark court in Fleet Street'. This was where Dickens' career began.

[If you are walking at the weekend, you can now reach the Temple by following Johnson's Court back down to Fleet Street. Turn left, then take a right down Bouverie Street, and then another right when you come to Tudor Street. This will lead you to the gatehouse, from which porters will admit you to the Temple grounds, although not the gardens.]

Johnson's Court, where Dickens first submitted a story to *The Monthly Magazine*.

A late-Victorian photograph of Fleet Street.

FOCUS ON: *THE STRAND*

The Strand was one of the most important thoroughfares in Dickens' London, linking government at Westminster and the fashionable world of Mayfair with the mercantile City. It was a peculiar street, because it belonged neither to the West End, nor to the world of business. It contained many shops, as well as hotels and theatres, and was proverbially busy, particularly before the creation of the Thames Embankment in the 1860s and Shaftesbury Avenue in the 1870s and 1880s, which finally created alternative east–west routes through the most central part of the metropolis. Some people were inspired by the constant bustle. The essayist Charles Lamb wrote to Wordsworth in 1801: 'I often shed tears in the motley Strand from fulness of joy at so much life.' It was this heavy foot traffic that also made it a nightly haunt for prostitutes, who made their way to its crowded pavements from the slums of Lambeth, on the opposite bank of the Thames.

It is difficult to picture its Dickensian character today. The author himself saw some of its old landmarks demolished in his lifetime. At the most westerly end of the road, the Golden Cross coaching inn, which appears in *The Pickwick Papers* and *David Copperfield*, was destroyed by the preparations for the building of Trafalgar Square in the 1830s. Likewise, Hungerford Market, a decaying collection of buildings on the site of the present Charing Cross station, was replaced in 1833 by a grand neo-classical development by Charles Fowler (which burned down in the 1850s, to be replaced by the present station in the 1860s). It was beside the old market that Dickens, at the age of twelve, was first obliged to work at Warren's blacking factory – the childhood humiliation he later confessed to his biographer John Forster.

One of the great attractions on the Strand was the Lowther Arcade, 'a covered walk or arcade, surmounted with glass domes of elegant design, leading from West Strand to St Martin's churchyard', similar to the Burlington Arcade, but chiefly populated by toy shops and sellers of expensive knick-knacks. It was situated opposite Villiers Street but did not belong to Dickens' childhood, having been built in

A late-Victorian photograph of the Strand.

1830. Dickens remembered it as the site of a pudding shop he frequented while at the blacking factory, selling 'stout, hale pudding, heavy and flabby; with great raisins in it'. The arcade was also adjacent to the Adelaide Gallery, combining 'scientific education' of paying customers with unlikely entertainments, including 'Perkins's steam gun, which discharges a stream of bullets at the rate of 1,000 in a minute' and 'the electrical eel in full life and vigour'. Further down the road, opposite Savoy Hill, there was another Strand landmark, the altogether less frivolous Exeter Hall. Built in the same period as the Lowther Arcade, this was a large classical meeting hall, extensively used by temperance societies, evangelicals and missionaries. Dickens knew it well and did not look upon it favourably. He was particularly opposed to missionaries working overseas, when faced with extensive poverty in England – hence Mrs Jellyby, the 'telescopic philanthropist' who neglects her own family in *Bleak House*. He would write in 1848, lambasting a venture in Niger, that 'whatever Exeter Hall champions is the thing by no means to be done'.

Both the Lowther Arcade and Exeter Hall were demolished in the Edwardian period, at the same time as a late-Victorian plan for the redevelopment of the Strand came to fruition: the creation of Kingsway and the Aldwych. These large new roads, wide European-style boulevards, swept away the most old-fashioned 'Dickensian' part of the Strand, between the churches of St Mary-le-Strand and St Clement Danes. It was here that the Strand narrowed, continuing along the south side of St Mary's, with a narrow lane, Holywell Street, running parallel to the north. The loss of Holywell Street was not much mourned, although it contained some very picturesque old timbered houses with quaint overhanging fronts. Holywell Street was the centre of Victorian London's pornography industry, 'a narrow dirty lane … occupied chiefly by old clothesmen and the vendors of low publications', with bookshops whose windows and front shelves were 'packed with vicious and gaudy literature, and other material, whose sort is hardly to be matched in the lowest quarters of Paris'. This was true even at the end of the nineteenth century, after numerous attempts to remove the pernicious material by the marvellously named 'Society for the Suppression of Vice'. Holywell Street was, therefore, conveniently flattened by the Aldwych – and a small piece of Dickens' London along with it.

A ROMANCE IN FOUNTAIN COURT
From *Martin Chuzzlewit*

There was a little plot between them, that Tom should always come out of the Temple by one way; and that was past the fountain. Coming through Fountain Court, he was just to glance down the steps leading into Garden Court, and to look once all round him; and if Ruth had come to meet him, there he would see her; not sauntering, you understand (on account of the clerks), but coming briskly up, with the best little laugh upon her face that ever played in opposition to the fountain, and beat it all to nothing. For, fifty to one, Tom had been looking for her in the wrong direction, and had quite given her up, while she had been tripping towards him from the first; jingling that little reticule of hers (with all the keys in it) to attract his wandering observation.

Whether there was life enough left in the slow vegetation of Fountain Court for the smoky shrubs to have any consciousness of the brightest and purest-hearted little woman in the world, is a question for gardeners, and those who are learned in the loves of plants. But, that it was a good thing for that same paved yard to have such a delicate little figure flitting through it; that it passed like a smile from the grimy old houses, and the worn flagstones, and left them duller, darker, sterner than before; there is no sort of doubt. The Temple fountain might have leaped up twenty feet to greet the spring of hopeful maidenhood, that in her person stole on, sparkling, through the dry and dusty channels of the Law; the chirping sparrows, bred in Temple chinks and crannies, might have held their peace to listen to imaginary skylarks, as so fresh a little creature passed; the dingy boughs, unused to droop, otherwise than in their puny growth, might have bent down in a kindred gracefulness to shed their benedictions on her graceful head; old love letters, shut up in iron boxes in the neighbouring offices, and made of no account among the heaps of family papers into which they had strayed, and of which, in their degeneracy, they formed a part, might have stirred and fluttered with a moment's recollection of their ancient tenderness, as she went lightly by. Anything might have happened that did not happen, and never will, for the love of Ruth.

Something happened, too, upon the afternoon of which the history treats. Not for her love. Oh no! quite by accident, and without the least reference to her at all.

Either she was a little too soon, or Tom was a little too late – she was so precise in general, that she timed it to half a minute – but no Tom was there. Well! But was anybody else there, that she blushed so deeply, after looking round, and tripped off down the steps with such unusual expedition?

Why, the fact is, that Mr Westlock was passing at that moment. The Temple is a public thoroughfare; they may write up on the gates that it is not, but so long as the gates are left open it is, and will be; and Mr Westlock had as good a right to be there as anybody else. But why did she run away, then? Not being ill dressed, for she was much too neat for that, why did she run away? The brown hair that had fallen down beneath her bonnet, and had one impertinent imp of a false flower clinging to it, boastful of its licence before all men, THAT could not have been the cause, for it looked charming. Oh! foolish, panting, frightened little heart, why did she run away!

Merrily the tiny fountain played, and merrily the dimples sparkled on its sunny face. John Westlock hurried after her.

WALK 4:
BLOOMSBURY AND KING'S CROSS

Starting location: Fitzroy Square, W1T 6AH.

Nearest tube station: Warren Street or Euston Square.

Walking time: 2 hours.

Opening hours:

- BRITISH MUSEUM: Monday, Wednesday, Thursday and Friday, 9.30 a.m. to 6 p.m.; Tuesday, 9.30 a.m. to 8 p.m.; Saturday, 9.30 a.m. to 5 p.m.; Sunday, 11 a.m. to 5 p.m.
- DICKENS HOUSE: Monday to Saturday, 10 a.m. to 5 p.m.; Sunday, 11 a.m. to 5 p.m.

W E BEGIN OUR WALK in Fitzroy Square, in the heart of 'Fitzrovia', a modern coinage for a rather obscure and neglected part of London, squeezed between Soho and the Euston Road. Dickens speaks of the square's 'barrenness and frigidity' in *Nicholas Nickleby*, an appraisal perhaps coloured by his own experience. It was in Fitzrovia that Dickens spent several of his teenage years, while his father, John Dickens, always struggling with his finances, moved the family from one temporary home to another. In one particular embarrassment, Dickens' mother made a brief, unsuccessful attempt to open a school in nearby Gower Street North, now the portion of Gower Street that adjoins Euston Square station. The young Dickens was obliged to circulate fliers in the surrounding district. He would later write: 'Nobody ever came to school, nor do I ever recollect that anybody ever proposed to come.' The family also lived in

Fitzroy Square: the family of John Dickens lived in Fitzroy Street in 1832–3.

Fitzroy Street itself, adjoining the square, in 1832–3. There was, however, one address in Fitzrovia at which the Dickens clan spent an unusually long spell of four years. To find it, we must head south.

Leave the square in the south-western corner and turn right on to Grafton Way, then left on to Cleveland Street. Keep walking until you pass Howland Street on the left. This area was once dominated by the Middlesex Hospital, whose site is now a vacant lot. The unprepossessing brick building on the left with two projecting wings, opposite Foley Street and the King and Queen pub, was an adjunct to the hospital. Originally, however, it served as a workhouse for the inhabitants of the parish of St Paul, Covent Garden (1778–1835), and then for the larger district covered by the Strand Poor Law Union (1836–67). It has been given Grade II listed status, in part because it may have served as inspiration for the workhouse in *Oliver Twist*. The novel's workhouse is actually located in an unnamed town north of

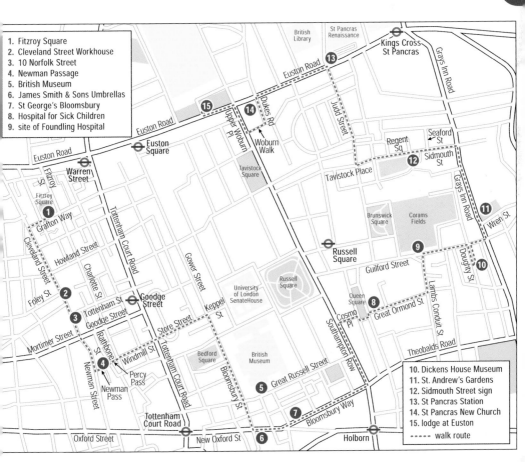

1. Fitzroy Square
2. Cleveland Street Workhouse
3. 10 Norfolk Street
4. Newman Passage
5. British Museum
6. James Smith & Sons Umbrellas
7. St George's Bloomsbury
8. Hospital for Sick Children
9. site of Foundling Hospital

10. Dickens House Museum
11. St. Andrew's Gardens
12. Sidmouth Street sign
13. St Pancras Station
14. St Pancras New Church
15. lodge at Euston
----- walk route

Middlesex Hospital, which stood opposite the Dickens family's rooms in 10 Norfolk Street (now 22 Cleveland Street).

London, but it is not unreasonable to make the suggestion, for the house in which the Dickens family lived between 1828 and 1832 lies only a few doors down the road, at 22 Cleveland Street, on the corner of Tottenham Street, formerly known as 10 Norfolk Street. The house belonged to John Dodd, a grocer, who had originally accommodated the Dickens family in 1815–16, when Dickens' father was first obliged to reside in London by his employers, the Navy Pay Office (this was a brief period in the capital, before another move, to Sheerness in Kent). The exterior is little changed, and it is clear that this was not impressive accommodation for a large family, bearing in mind that John Dickens had five surviving children in 1828, in addition to young Charles. Dodd, in turn, would become one of John Dickens' many creditors.

The Dickensian alleyway of Newman Passage.

Keep going along Cleveland Street, cross over where Goodge Street meets Mortimer Street, and go down Newman Street. Somewhere on this road is Mr Turveydrop's dancing academy in *Bleak House*, 'a sufficiently dingy house at the corner of an archway'. This 'archway' might refer to Newman Passage, a suitably Dickensian alley that slopes down between Nos. 27 and 26. Follow the alley and go down the covered walk that leads straight on, past the side door of the Newman Arms (established 1860) on to Rathbone Street. Percy Passage, a continuation of the alley, can be seen on the other side of the road. Follow it through on to Charlotte Street, then turn left and immediately right, along Windmill Street. Keep straight on until you come to the Rising Sun pub on the corner of Tottenham Court Road. We are somewhere in the vicinity of the shop of the 'ornamental stationer and small circulating library keeper', brother to the awful Miss Knag in *Nicholas Nickleby*, its precise location left rather vague in the book, and a short walk from the broker's shop 'up at the top of Tottenham Court Road', where Traddles's furniture ends up, having been repossessed by bailiffs in *David Copperfield* (echoes of Dickens' own debt-ridden father).

Young David Copperfield, Dickens' *alter ego*, demands 'your best – your very best – ale' from a publican.

WALK 4

Cross the road, and head down Store Street. At the end of the road, on the far side of Gower Street, leading up to the Art Deco skyscraper of Senate House (the administrative centre of the University of London) is Keppel Street. It was here that John Dickens died on 30 March 1851, at the house of his doctor, Robert Davey. In his later years he was, inevitably, supported financially by his somewhat reluctant son. His death occurred five days after a perilous and anaesthetic-free operation on his bladder. We know Dickens himself was present at his bedside along with several members of his family, as it was the night of the 1851 census.

Do not proceed down Keppel Street, but turn right down Gower Street, along the eastern side of Bedford Square, to the junction with Great Russell Street. Look left and you will see the railings of the British Museum. Dickens first obtained a reader's ticket to use the

LIFE PRESERVERS, DAGGER CANES, SWORDSTICKS.

One of the ornate signs at James Smith & Sons' umbrella shop.

WALK 4

museum's library at the age of eighteen, while living in Norfolk Street. You may wish to take a diversion down Great Russell Street and explore the museum's many treasures. The museum's library is now the British Library at St Pancras. You can, however, still see the famous circular Reading Room in the heart of the old museum, built in 1854–7, twenty-five years after Dickens' first visit.

Continue down Bloomsbury Street to its junction with New Oxford Street. On the opposite side of the road you will see the unmistakeable Victorian frontage of James Smith & Sons' umbrella shop. This unusual family business dates to 1830, and the New Oxford Street shop to 1857. The giant projecting lettering above the ground floor – 'Jas. Smith & Sons Umbrellas' – is typical of West End shops of the period, right down to the abbreviation of James as 'Jas'. The shop's interior also contains many original fittings.

Facing the umbrella shop, turn left and walk to the end of New Oxford Street. Then, where the road splits, keep left down Bloomsbury Way. You will pass the church of St George, designed by the brilliant, eccentric architect Nicholas Hawksmoor, completed in 1731. The unique stepped tower is based on Pliny the Elder's description of the Mausoleum of Halicarnassus and is topped by a statue of George I in Roman dress. Around the base of the tower are fighting lions and unicorns, a symbol of George's triumph over the Jacobite uprising; these are recent restorations, the originals having been removed in the 1870s. The church is the venue for the 'Bloomsbury Christening' in Dickens' *Sketches by Boz*.

A lion chases a unicorn on the distinctive Hawksmoor spire of St George's, Bloomsbury.

Continue up Bloomsbury Way, then turn left down Southampton Row. Cross over and look for a small pedestrianised turning, Cosmo Place. This will lead you into Queen Square, which contains a number of London hospitals. Dickens knew several of the founders of these institutions, including Frederic Hervey

Foster Quin, the charismatic physician who set up the London Homeopathic Hospital (the current hospital building dates from 1895–1911, on the south-eastern corner of Queen Square), and Charles West, who established the Hospital for Sick Children (now better known as Great Ormond Street Hospital), which opened in 1852. Dickens was a staunch supporter of the latter, marking its launch in his magazine *Household Words* with an article entitled 'Drooping Buds'. The title may sound sentimental but Dickens does not hesitate to note that 'Of all the coffins that are made in London, more than one in every three is made for a little child'. The article also contains an interesting description of the square as 'cut off from the life of the town – in London but not of it – a suburb left between the New Road (Euston Road) and High Holborn'. That atmosphere lingers today. Dickens even mentions the square's solitary water pump, which still remains in place.

Leave the square via Great Ormond Street, past the modern Hospital for Sick Children. Turn left at the junction with Lamb's Conduit Street. At the end of the street, you can see the wall and gate of Coram's Fields, where the Foundling Hospital used to stand

The original Great Ormond Street Hospital, which first opened in 1852.

The Dickens House Museum, 48 Doughty Street.

Tombstones piled against a wall in St Andrew's Gardens.

(the site is now a children's playground). This institution, established in 1742, took in unwanted children and educated them, often sending boys to the army and girls into service. Dickens was, again, a public supporter of the charity (he wrote 'Received, a Blank Child' in *Household Words* in 1853) and regularly worshipped at its chapel while living in Bloomsbury. The headstrong Tattycoram of *Little Dorrit* is one of its 'foundling-girls', as is the central figure in *No Thoroughfare*, the mystery co-written with Wilkie Collins in 1867.

Turn right down Guilford Street, and take the third right to Doughty Street. Number 48 is the Dickens House Museum, Dickens' only surviving family home in London, where he moved a year after his marriage to Catherine Hogarth. His literary success meant that he was able to move to a much larger property near Regent's Park in 1839; yet it was here in Doughty Street that he established himself in the literary firmament, finishing *The Pickwick Papers*, and writing both *Oliver Twist* and *Nicholas Nickleby*.

If you have time, you should explore the Dickens House Museum. When you have finished, retrace your route up Doughty Street, and then turn right on Guilford Street, to the junction with Gray's Inn Road. Mr Casby in *Little Dorrit* lives in this district; and Mr Micawber of *David Copperfield* also has lodgings hereabouts. Turn left and you will see, on the opposite side of Gray's Inn Road, just after Wren Street, a pair of ornate ironwork gates. If you cross over and go inside, you will find a small public garden, replete with chest-like tombs and gravestones piled haphazardly along the walls. This is St Andrew's Gardens, one of London's many old burial grounds (belonging to St Andrew's, Holborn), which, having become

Mr Micawber, whom Dickens modelled on his debt-ridden father.

full to bursting by the mid-nineteenth century, were closed to burials in the 1840s and 1850s, and either redeveloped, or redesigned as parks and gardens. It is such a burial ground that Dickens describes in *Bleak House* ('a dreadful spot in which the night was very slowly stirring, but where I could dimly see heaps of dishonoured graves and stones, hemmed in by filthy houses with a few dull lights in their windows and on whose walls a thick humidity broke out like a disease'). It was not uncommon for such places to have bodies buried six or seven deep, one coffin on top of another, so close to the surface that remains could be exposed by animals or erosion of the soil.

The miserable, disease-ridden old burial ground of *Bleak House*.

Leave the gardens and continue along Gray's Inn Road until you see Sidmouth Street, and turn left. Most of the buildings here are modern, but past Seaford Street you will notice some older houses on the left. There is an entrance to another burial ground (St George's Gardens) but, a few yards further on, round the side of No. 55 is a rare survival – several overlapping layers of painted Victorian street advertisements, touting the wares of a local chemist.

The Gothic interior of the Midland Grand Hotel, St Pancras.

Old street advertisements revealed in overlapping layers of paint.

Painted advertisements were commonplace on the sides of Victorian buildings, as well as fly-posting. Advertisers would hire gangs of painters who sought out sites, daubing their neatly lettered graffiti on any available surface, without the owners' approval.

Continue to the end of Sidmouth Street, then turn right down Judd Street. At the end of the road, a dramatic spectacle awaits you: the Midland Grand Hotel (now the St Pancras Renaissance), fronting St Pancras station. It is perhaps a little suspect to include it within a Dickens guidebook, but it was planned in Dickens' lifetime (begun in 1868; opened to the public in 1873) and is the greatest triumph of Victorian Gothic in London. It fell into decay and disrepair in the twentieth century, but it has been magnificently restored, inside and out. It even has its own hotel historian, who offers tours of the building.

Turn left along Euston Road, formerly the 'New Road'. There is another fascinating spectacle at the junction with Duke's Road – St Pancras New Church, built between 1819 and 1822, the earliest

Greek Revival church in London. Its most unmissable features are the sets of caryatids (giant female figures, supporting the roof), modelled on the Erechtheion temple on the Acropolis in Athens. Dickens' daughter Mary was christened here in 1837; and we are also a short distance from the site of Tavistock House, where the Dickens family lived in the 1850s (now the site of the British Medical Association's building in Tavistock Square). While you are passing, it is worth taking a glance at the bow-windowed shops of Duke's Road and Woburn Walk, designed by the master builder Thomas Cubitt in 1822. They are impressively well preserved and have made numerous film and television appearances, standing in for various parts of Victorian London.

Our final destination lies after the junction with Upper Woburn Place, on the opposite side of the road from the church. Euston is the oldest main-line station in the capital,

The caryatids of St Pancras New Church.

Georgian shops in Duke's Place and Woburn Walk.

WALK 4

WALK 4

One of the classical lodges of the original Euston station.

opened in 1837. At its entrance was once a grand Doric arch, destroyed in an infamous act of cultural vandalism during the 1960s, together with the station buildings, including the 1849 Great Hall, the station's main booking hall, also in the classical style – more like the interior of a Greek temple than a railway station, with elaborate mouldings and vast coffered ceiling. All that remains now is a pair of classical 'lodges' on the Euston Road (currently being used as bars for busy commuters). It is from Euston that the grim, money-loving Mr Dombey and wily Major Bagstock set forth for a refreshing holiday in Leamington Spa. The station is not specified but it can be nowhere else. You can check this yourself. A quick glance at the lodges will reveal that 'Leamington' is one of the destinations etched into the lodges' walls – an unusual form of permanent advertisement, the history of the railway written in stone.

The approach to Euston station in the nineteenth century.

FOCUS ON: *KING'S CROSS*

The district of King's Cross is now known for its twin railway stations, King's Cross (built 1851–2) and St Pancras (1863–7), which dominate the Euston Road. The name of King's Cross derives from a 60-foot-tall octagonal building, topped with a statue of George IV, which stood opposite the site of the station between 1830 and 1845. It was a monument to the monarch, but its interior also served several purposes in its lifetime, including 'a place of exhibition, then a police-station, and last of all a beer-shop'. It was never a popular memorial and was removed as an obstruction to traffic, leaving only its name behind. The old name for the district was Battle Bridge, referring to a ford over the long-buried Fleet River, which once ran the length of Gray's Inn Road – this is the name you will see consistently in Dickens' works. The area is prominent in *Our Mutual Friend*, but not for its railways or even the towering ironwork gasholders that were erected in the 1850s and recently demolished (awaiting resurrection incorporated into a new housing development). Instead, Dickens describes Battle Bridge as 'a tract of suburban Sahara, where tiles and bricks were burnt, bones were boiled, carpets were beat, rubbish was shot, dogs were fought, and dust was heaped by contractors' – in other words, home to all the dirtiest trades in London, including the dust-yard (rubbish and recycling dump) central to his plot.

The land behind the railway stations were certainly a blighted region. A letter to *The Times* in 1855 complains of the pervasive 'exhalations of the bone-boiling, and the smells of the patent manufactory, and the smells of the horse-slaughtering house, beaten down by the wind', ruining gardens and afflicting local children with bouts of 'nausea and violent retching'. An 1870s visitor describes children improvising a ball game on 'a tolerably level bit between two dust-heaps'. The writer continues, rather gruesomely: 'for wickets they had a pile of old hats and broken crockery; for bat the stump leg of an old bedstead, and for ball the head of a kitten'. The dust-heaps were

The Regent's Canal, and the last King's Cross gasholder undergoing demolition.

WALK 4

WALK 4

certainly the most visible signs of these troublesome industries, large hillocks of rubbish, consisting principally of ashes and cinders collected by dustmen, together with other objects that made their way into Londoners' dustbins, from broken crockery to food waste. Virtually all of these items had some recycling value: ashes and cinders were used in brickmaking; the so-called 'hard-ware' of 'broken pottery, pans, crockery, earthenware, oyster-shells &c.' were used as a foundation for roads; 'soft-ware' – anything that might decompose – was sold as manure. Dead cats were a regular sight – hence the rather horrible description above – and even they had their price: dealers in fur offered 'sixpence for a white cat, fourpence for a colored cat, and for a black one according to her quality'.

Recycling meant there was money in 'dust', and hence a large contingent of sifters worked the dustyards, sorting through all the refuse by hand. These were women and children, the families of the dustmen who went round collecting the refuse. The owners of the yards and the contractors who employed the dustmen could make large profits. It is likely that the portrayal of Boffin in *Our Mutual Friend* was inspired by the real-life dustyard owner and brickmaker Henry Dodd, who built his business from scratch and met Dickens through their mutual interest in setting up an actors' charity. The value of dust, however, diminished during the nineteenth century, as new brickmaking methods were introduced. Contractors who had once paid local parishes for the privilege of collecting waste now demanded to be paid for their services.

It is difficult to direct visitors to the site of the dust-heaps today, as the King's Cross area is in a large-scale redevelopment project, so that roads are regularly closed and access routes changed. You should, however, be able to walk up Pancras Road, on the King's Cross side of St Pancras station. This will eventually bring you to the gates of St Pancras Old Church on the right. The church may be one of the oldest Christian sites in Europe, with a Saxon altar discovered, dating from AD 600. It is here that Dickens sets the body-snatching scene in *A Tale of Two Cities*. If you leave the churchyard by the rear exit and turn left along Camley Street, you will come to steps leading down to the Regent's Canal. Turn left on to the towpath, and you can walk through the same King's Cross hinterlands that Dickens describes, along the canal route that once transported Mr Boffin's dust to the brickmakers' yards.

THE DANCING ACADEMY IN NEWMAN STREET

From *Bleak House*

Caddy went on to say with considerable hesitation and reluctance that there was one thing more she wished us to know, and felt we ought to know, and which she hoped would not offend us. It was that she had improved her acquaintance with Miss Flite, the little crazy old lady, and that she frequently went there early in the morning and met her lover for a few minutes before breakfast – only for a few minutes. 'I go there at other times,' said Caddy, 'but Prince does not come then. Young Mr Turveydrop's name is Prince; I wish it wasn't, because it sounds like a dog, but of course he didn't christen himself. Old Mr Turveydrop had him christened Prince in remembrance of the Prince Regent. Old Mr Turveydrop adored the Prince Regent on account of his deportment. I hope you won't think the worse of me for having made these little appointments at Miss Flite's, where I first went with you, because I like the poor thing for her own sake and I believe she likes me. If you could see young Mr Turveydrop, I am sure you would think well of him – at least, I am sure you couldn't possibly think any ill of him. I am going there now for my lesson. I couldn't ask you to go with me, Miss Summerson; but if you would,' said Caddy, who had said all this earnestly and tremblingly, 'I should be very glad – very glad.'

It happened that we had arranged with my guardian to go to Miss Flite's that day. We had told him of our former visit, and our account had interested him; but something had always happened to prevent our going there again. As I trusted that I might have sufficient influence with Miss Jellyby to prevent her taking any very rash step if I fully accepted the confidence she was so willing to place in me, poor girl, I proposed that she and I and Peepy should go to the academy and afterwards meet my guardian and Ada at Miss Flite's, whose name I now learnt for the first time. This was on condition that Miss Jellyby and Peepy should come back with us to dinner. The last article of the agreement being joyfully acceded to by both, we smartened Peepy up a little with the assistance of a few pins, some

**The Turveydrop
dancing academy in
Bleak House.**

soap and water, and a hair-brush, and went out, bending our steps towards
Newman Street, which was very near.

I found the academy established in a sufficiently dingy house at the
corner of an archway, with busts in all the staircase windows. In the same
house there were also established, as I gathered from the plates on the door,
a drawing-master, a coal-merchant (there was, certainly, no room for his
coals), and a lithographic artist. On the plate which, in size and situation,
took precedence of all the rest, I read, MR TURVEYDROP. The door was open,
and the hall was blocked up by a grand piano, a harp, and several other
musical instruments in cases, all in progress of removal, and all looking
rakish in the daylight. Miss Jellyby informed me that the academy had
been lent, last night, for a concert.

We went upstairs – it had been quite a fine house once, when it was
anybody's business to keep it clean and fresh, and nobody's business to
smoke in it all day – and into Mr Turveydrop's great room, which was built
out into a mews at the back and was lighted by a skylight. It was a bare,
resounding room smelling of stables, with cane forms along the walls, and
the walls ornamented at regular intervals with painted lyres and little cut-
glass branches for candles, which seemed to be shedding their old-fashioned
drops as other branches might shed autumn leaves. Several young lady
pupils, ranging from thirteen or fourteen years of age to two or three and
twenty, were assembled; and I was looking among them for their instructor
when Caddy, pinching my arm, repeated the ceremony of introduction.
'Miss Summerson, Mr Prince Turveydrop!'

WALK 5:
HOLBORN

Tip: To get the most out of this walk and follow the route effectively, a weekday lunchtime is essential (see opening hours, below).

Starting location: Fleet Street, EC4A 2HR.

Nearest tube station: Temple or Chancery Lane.

Walking time: 1¼ hours.

Opening hours:

- LINCOLN'S INN, STAPLE INN: Monday to Friday only, *not at all at weekends*.
- GRAY'S INN: Monday to Friday only, 12 noon to 2.30 p.m.
- JOHN SOANE MUSEUM: Tuesday to Saturday, 10 a.m. to 5 p.m.

O N THE NORTH SIDE of Fleet Street, beside the church of St Dunstan-in-the-West, lies a seemingly nondescript alley. Yet it contains an old gatehouse – the entrance to Clifford's Inn, which was demolished in the 1930s – a threshold we shall cross, to start a journey that will take us through the legal quarter of Dickens' London.

If you have already spent time in the Inner and Middle Temple (on the opposite side of Fleet Street, see Walk 3) then you will have already visited two of the four Inns of Court, the medieval colleges that still play a part in a barrister's legal education. While the Temple presents a bewildering array of quadrangles, gardens and courtyards, Clifford's Inn, on the other hand, was much smaller – a single courtyard and surrounding buildings – one of the Inns of Chancery. These lesser inns began in the fifteenth century as preparatory schools for the larger Inns of Court, and later lost their educational function, becoming professional associations and social clubs to which solicitors and attorneys could attach themselves (the Inns of Court being reserved for barristers). They were quaint, somewhat obsolete institutions even in Dickens' time, but still providing lodgings and office space for lawyers. The great author seems to have enjoyed their curiosity value and Clifford's Inn appears in several of his novels. This alley is the spot where Rokesmith takes Mr Boffin, leading him away from the bustle of Fleet Street, to propose becoming his secretary in *Our Mutual Friend*. The idle Tip Dorrit also finds brief paid employment in Clifford's Inn – 'a stool and twelve shillings a week' in an attorney's office – an echo there of Dickens' dissatisfaction with his own brief spell of work as a law clerk in the 1820s.

Go through the gate. On your left is the former site of another of the Inns of Chancery, Serjeant's Inn. This was a rather cramped building that once housed the Court of Common Pleas – the place where Mr Pickwick has his trial. Serjeant's Inn was demolished in 1910, but a surviving Victorian masterpiece lies immediately ahead of you – the

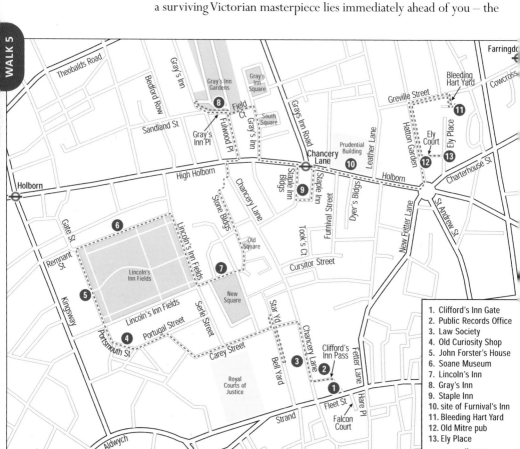

1. Clifford's Inn Gate
2. Public Records Office
3. Law Society
4. Old Curiosity Shop
5. John Forster's House
6. Soane Museum
7. Lincoln's Inn
8. Gray's Inn
9. Staple Inn
10. site of Furnival's Inn
11. Bleeding Hart Yard
12. Old Mitre pub
13. Ely Place
----- walk route

former Public Records Office, now part of the campus of King's College London. The building is a marvellous, sturdy example of neo-Gothic by James Pennethorne. It was built in the 1850s and 1860s as a secure repository for the nation's historic records relating to law and government, documents formerly scattered in locations from the Tower of London to Westminster Abbey.

Turn left and the path takes you towards Chancery Lane. Opposite is the Law Society, the professional body for solicitors. The Society was founded in the 1820s, its formal title being 'The Society of Attorneys, Solicitors, Proctors and others not being Barristers, practising in the Courts of Law and Equity of the United Kingdom'. It opened the impressive Chancery Lane building in 1832. The Society was determined to improve professional standards and its early activities included prosecuting corrupt lawyers and, in the 1860s, bringing in a system of formal examinations. Dickens' damning portrayal of the profession in *Bleak House* is well known. The labyrinthine Chancery case, with its long-promised inheritance, is a profitable business for a host of legal parasites, and poison to its supposed beneficiaries. Nonetheless, in the interests of balance, we must note that it was the Victorian members

Above left: An impression of Serjeant's Inn, Chancery Lane, in the eighteenth century (demolished 1910).

Above right: The gatehouse to Clifford's Inn survived the Inn's demolition in 1934.

The headquarters of the Law Society, Chancery Lane, opened in 1832.

The Gothic clock attached to the Public Records Office.

of the Law Society who began the process of creating a regulated modern legal profession.

Turn right on Chancery Lane itself. Just after the Public Records Office is an undistinguished modern office block. This is the site of Symonds Inn, one of three locations where Dickens worked as a clerk in 1827 and 1828, and also the location of the offices of the crafty Vholes in *Bleak House*. We shall, however, turn away from Chancery Lane for now, and head left along Carey Street, next to the Law Society building. On the left is Bell Yard, the home of the Blinders in *Bleak House*. It is worth a brief diversion to look at the quaint miniature firemen's busts in a rear doorway of the Law Society (as part of a building that once belonged to the Law Fire Insurance Office). You may also wish to make a brief diversion down Star Yard, on the opposite side of Carey Street. A little way down the street, there is a peculiar green structure propped against the left-hand wall – one of the last surviving Victorian *pissoirs* in London (although long since closed to the public).

Return to Carey Street and continue along it. On your right is a gateway to Lincoln's Inn, one of the four Inns of Court, to which we shall return in due course; on your left is the back of the Royal Courts of Justice – another marvellous Gothic building, but from after Dickens' time, built in the 1870s in a district that was formerly slum housing.

WALK 5

Follow Carey Street to its conclusion, as it bends round to the right, then take a left down Portugal Street. Here, on the north side of the road, stood the Court for the Relief of Insolvent Debtors, chronicled in *The Pickwick Papers* and *Little Dorrit* ('understood, by the general consent of all the destitute shabby-genteel people in London, as their common resort, and place of daily refuge'), which also reviewed the finances of Dickens' impecunious father in both 1824 and 1831.

We are pointing out, perhaps, too many long-vanished places. There is, however, something more tangible just around the corner. Turn right into Portsmouth Steet, and you will see a tumbledown building of genuine antiquity that proclaims itself – in Gothic script above the door – as 'The Old Curiosity Shop, Immortalised by Charles Dickens'. The building, restored in the 1880s, is undoubtedly old, possibly the oldest shop in London, dating to the sixteenth century, but, unfortunately, it has no connection to Dickens. The house bears no relation to the description in the book, which itself concludes with a statement that 'The old house had been long ago pulled down, and a fine broad road was in its place'. Moreover, a relative of the owner of the shop in the 1880s was happy to state that the Dickens link was invented by his brother-in-law in the previous decade 'for purely business purposes, as likely to attract custom to his shop, he being a dealer in books, paintings, old china and so on'. It has been so long established as a Dickens landmark, despite its dubious claims to authenticity, that the building is unlikely to be removed from the tourist map.

The Old Curiosity Shop, Portsmouth Street, is not the building described by Dickens. Its Dickensian connection was entirely the invention of a former proprietor.

At the end of Portsmouth Street, you approach the south-western corner of Lincoln's Inn Fields, a square developed in the seventeenth century. To the right is the grand classical home of the Royal College of Surgeons (designed by Charles Barry in the 1830s, rebuilt and extended after bombing in the Second World War). Carry on straight ahead, however, past the New Academic Building of

the London School of Economics, and you will see Nos. 57 and 58 Lincoln's Inn Fields. The square was once largely residential in character and Dickens knew No. 58 as the home of the literary and dramatic critic John Forster, his intimate friend and biographer. The house also forms the model for the house of Tulkinghorn, the Machiavellian lawyer in *Bleak House*. It is here that the cold-hearted Tulkinghorn, 'a hard-grained man, close, dry, and silent', sits at his open window on a warm evening with a bottle of old port, 'pondering at that twilight hour on all the mysteries he knows'. Betsey Trotwood of *David Copperfield* also stays in a hotel nearby, although it is impossible to pinpoint its location.

At the north-east corner of the square, where it is met by Remnant Street, turn right to remain in Lincoln's Inn Fields. Watch out for No. 13, the home of the architect John Soane (1753–1837). Soane left the house to the nation, and it remains virtually untouched, a museum containing a vast collection of curiosities, art and antiques amassed during his lifetime (including the original canvases of Hogarth's *A Rake's Progress*, and an Egyptian sarcophagus in the basement). The interior is not typical: it is actually three houses combined into one, with various unique features designed to showcase the art and sculpture. The principal rooms at the front of the house, however, may provide some clue to how the home of Forster or Tulkinghorn would have looked in Dickens' day.

The house in Lincoln's Inn Fields belonging to Dickens' friend and biographer John Forster.

Continue past Soane's House and turn right at the corner of the square. On your left is the wall of Lincoln's Inn (the Inn of Court, as distinct from Lincoln's Inn Fields), and behind it lies another stunning piece of Victorian Gothic, the Great Hall (or New Hall), designed by Philip Charles Hardwick, and built in 1843–5 for the Inn's members. It was opened by Queen Victoria and remains as a grand dining hall (would-be barristers must attend several formal dinners there as part of the qualification for being 'called to the bar'), as well as a venue for meetings and concerts. Just past the hall is the Inn's principal gatehouse, which dates from the same period: it is here that we shall enter the inn itself.

Like the Temple, Lincoln's Inn contains a variety of squares and courtyards. It is particularly rich in ornate and unusual vintage gaslights, which create a mysterious and enchanting atmosphere on a winter's evening. You will notice New Square on the right, whose gateway we passed in Carey Street, a square that dates from the late

The lawyer in *Bleak House*, Mr Tulkinghorn (left), who lived in Lincoln's Inn Fields.

seventeenth century. The building immediately ahead of you is the Old Hall of the Inn, completed in 1492; it is also the setting for the Court of Chancery hearings in *Bleak House*. The Old Hall is next to the Inn's chapel, and if you walk through the covered passage between them you can see the chapel's extraordinary vaulted undercroft to the left. Behind the Old Hall is the gateway to Chancery Lane, the principal entrance to the Inn before the 1840s.

Old Square lies next to the chapel (take a left turn, if you are approaching it from the Lincoln's Inn Fields gatehouse); here the lawyers in Jarndyce v Jarndyce have their chambers in *Bleak House*, and likewise Serjeant Snubbins, the barrister retained by Perker in *The Pickwick Papers*. Walk past Old Square and you will come to Stone Buildings. This square appears to be a dead end, but head for the far corner, on the right, and you will find a narrow passage leading through to Chancery Lane.

An antique gaslight (now running on electricity) in Lincoln's Inn.

A good deal of the action in *Bleak House* takes place in this street. We learn early on in the novel that 'old Tom Jarndyce in despair blew his brains out at a coffee-house in Chancery Lane'. We have already mentioned Mr Vholes' chambers, and if you wish to turn right and go back down the lane, you will pass Cursitor Street and Took's Court ('Cook's Court') on the left – the site of Mr Snagsby's Law Stationers. Further down on the right stands Chichester Rents, the site of the

The southern gate to Lincoln's Inn.

Sol's Arms public house, where a coroner's inquest takes place; Krook's rag and bottle warehouse is also somewhere in this vicinity. Both locations, however, lack much in the way of surviving buildings, so we suggest a left turn from Lincoln's Inn to the top of Chancery Lane. Cross over the main thoroughfare of High Holborn, turn right, then take the first left down the narrow walk of Fulwood Place. This will bring you into the most northerly of the Inns of Court, Gray's Inn.

Immediately ahead, you will see the garden walks for which the inn is most famous, laid out by Sir Francis Bacon in 1606. Gray's Inn was where the young Dickens spent most of his time as a law clerk, in the offices of Ellis and Blackmore. The second of these offices was in the terrace called Raymond Buildings, built in the 1820s, shortly before Dickens' arrival. To see this terrace, turn left from Fulwood Place, and then right, between the buildings in Gray's Inn Place. Raymond Buildings is the end of the long row of houses ahead of you, facing the outer wall of the Inn.

A hand-painted sign; note the direction 'manicule' used in Victorian signage.

Now double back. Pass Fulwood Place on your right, and then turn right into South Square. You will see the ivy-covered eastern side of the square and a statue of Sir Francis

Bacon. This was the first place in which Dickens worked as a clerk, and was formerly known as Holborn Court. Unsurprisingly, Gray's Inn also features in Dickens' novels – it is the home of the lawyer Perker and the barrister Mr Phunky in *The Pickwick Papers*, and of Traddles in *David Copperfield* (No. 2 Holborn Court). Flora Finching of *Little Dorrit* also contemplates a tryst with Arthur Clenham – never to be realised – in Gray's Inn Gardens.

You can exit South Square on the right, leading to an arched gateway back on to High Holborn. Turn left, then look for Staple Inn Buildings on the far side of the road, behind the entrance to Chancery Lane tube station. Cross over and head down this pedestrianised street. Turn left through the gateway into an ornamental garden. This is Staple Inn, another Inn of Chancery, which features prominently in Dickens' uncompleted *Edwin Drood*, as the chambers of Mr Grewgious. The garden's doorway and fountain are described in the novel, and, if you go past the fountain and turn left into the second courtyard of the Inn, this is the quiet spot 'turning into which out of the clashing street, imparts to the relieved pedestrian the sensation of having put cotton in his ears, and velvet soles on his boots'. We, however, shall return to the busy street through the archway into

Below left: Arthur Clenham and the simpering Flora Finching (based on Dickens' erstwhile love, Maria Beadnell) in *Little Dorrit*.

Below: The rose garden in Staple Inn, as mentioned in *Edwin Drood*.

WALK 5

Holborn Bars. Above you, providing a façade for the Inn, is a row of Tudor half-timbered shops that survived the Great Fire of London.

Cross Holborn and walk over to the palatial, Gothic red-brick and terracotta building a hundred yards to the east. This was the offices of the Prudential Assurance Company, designed in the 1870s by Alfred Waterhouse (who was also the architect of the Natural History Museum) but altered and extended in the early twentieth century. It postdates Dickens but this was once the site of another Inn of Chancery, Furnival's Inn, in which the author rented rooms between 1834 and 1837 – it was here that he both embarked upon his marriage and began *The Pickwick Papers*. It is worth taking a stroll into the open square inside, to admire the building's ornate brickwork and tiling. There is a bust of Dickens in an alcove in the north-western corner, but it is a rather shoddy affair, almost invisible behind a perspex screen.

Leave the Prudential, retracing your steps, and then continue towards Holborn Circus and the equestrian statue of Prince Albert, erected in 1874. This area is also rich in Dickensian associations, although there is little for the modern observer to notice. Next to Leather Lane, on your left, stood the Bull coaching inn, where

The houses above Staple Inn survived the Great Fire of London.

Mrs Gamp of *Martin Chuzzlewit* has occasional work. On the opposite side of the road, a little down from Staple Inn, was Barnard's Inn, where Pip and Pocket room together in *Great Expectations*. Its 'dingiest collection of shabby buildings ever squeezed together in a rank corner as a club for Tom-cats' has long since disappeared, but a much restored Tudor dining hall still survives. Thavies Inn used to adjoin the top of New Fetter Lane, the home of misguided philanthropist Mrs. Jellby in *Bleak House*.

Turn left down Hatton Garden (where the Jellybys move, after their bankruptcy), then right down Greville Street. On the right you will see an entrance to Bleeding Heart Yard, the site of Daniel Doyce's factory ('heavily beating like a bleeding heart of iron, with the clink of metal upon metal') and the Plornishes' lodgings in *Little Dorrit*. The yard itself is much changed; the converted warehouses are late Victorian; and there is no sign of the steps which Dickens describes as leading down to it, nor of the low gateway out. Nevertheless, its confined boundaries remain unaltered and still evoke something of old London.

Retrace your steps along Hatton Garden, looking out for the narrow alley of Ely Court on the left, which leads to the Ye Olde Mitre Tavern. The pub has no direct Dickens connection, but it is ancient —

Below left: The Old Mitre public house, just off Ely Place.

Below: Ely Place was a private, gated road, with its own watch-house.

WALK 5

there was first a pub on this site in 1546 – and the small panelled rooms comprise the sort of old public house that would have been very familiar to the great novelist. Then continue through the alley and you will arrive at Ely Place.

Ely Place has a long history, with the land first belonging to the Bishops of Ely in the thirteenth century, then reverting to the Crown in 1772, when the present road was first laid out. It was a private road and is technically still under the aegis of a body of commissioners established by an 1842 local Act of Parliament – hence the presence of a gated watch-house at its principal entrance. It is in Ely Place that Agnes Wickfield stays with her father's legal agent, Mr Waterbook, in *David Copperfield*; and it is here that David stands, glancing nervously at the clock of St Andrew's Church – which still can be seen, across Holborn Viaduct – before summoning up the courage to ring Mr Waterbrook's bell and apologise for his drunken behaviour at the theatre. And it is at Mr Waterbrook's door, somewhere among these well-kept Georgian houses, that we finish our walk.

FOCUS ON: *HATTON GARDEN*

The district between Gray's Inn and Smithfield, now famous for the jewellers of Hatton Garden, was once at the heart of one of the worst slums of the capital. It is here that Dickens places Fagin's den in Field Lane (see Walk 6), and likewise the magistrates' court at which Oliver Twist looks set to receive little mercy from the irksome Mr Fang. Fang was based on a real Hatton Garden magistrate, called Laing, with a similar reputation for self-importance, intemperance and summary justice. Dickens noted, while writing the book, that he was 'casting about for a magistrate whose harshness and insolence would render him a fit subject to be shown up' and successfully persuaded a court reporter to get him 'smuggled into the Hatton garden office for a few moments some morning' to take notes.

The greatest example of continuity between past and present in the area is probably the street market in Leather Lane. In Dickens' time, admittedly, the modern take-aways and cafés would have been 'coffee-houses' partitioned into wooden booths, though still selling tea, coffee and cheap fried

Furnival's Inn, where Dickens lived between 1834 and 1837.

food. The hungry Victorian worker might also have turned to one of several varieties of street food, sold *al fresco*: fried fish, hot eels and pea soup, muffins and crumpets, or even oysters (a common snack, which could be had for 6d a dozen). The current market, with its random mixture of cheap and cheerful goods laid upon barrows, does not much differ from its nineteenth-century predecessor. The only thing missing is the cheap hawkers who once spread out their goods on cloths on the pavement.

Picturing the slums themselves is more difficult, amid the late-Victorian and more modern buildings that have replaced them. The early-Victorian

A sketch of Leather Lane.

'rookeries' were largely composed of decaying, poorly maintained houses that could never survive the nineteenth century, and some were even more temporary affairs. Brooke Market, for example, now an obscure, shady square behind the Prudential Assurance Building, just to the west of Leather Lane, contained 'a row of weather-board hovels, daubed with rusty tar, of almost as primitive construction as Canadian log-huts'. The square was principally inhabited by chimney-sweeps and 'scavengers' (dustmen, street cleaners and the like), one of the many examples in the Victorian metropolis of particular professions congregating in the same area. The church of St Alban the Martyr was built in Brooke Street in the early 1860s, adjacent to the square, specifically to spread religion among these slum folk. It was an uphill struggle, in a district that contained not only a good deal of criminality but numerous brothels. An 1850s visitor to the area describes the interiors of local lodging houses, with parlours and kitchens 'resembling the tap-room of a low public house' and containing 'some of the worst characters in London … men and women sitting, conversing, and smoking – using the most disgusting conversation'. Another guidebook from the same period notes of Saffron Hill that 'The clergymen of St Andrew's, Holborn, (the parish in which the purlieu lies), have been obliged, when visiting it, to be accompanied by policemen in plain clothes'. The poor reputation of Saffron Hill and its surrounds, which Dickens sealed in *Oliver Twist*, would persist until the end of the nineteenth century.

WALK 5

ACCOMMODATION IN BARNARD'S INN
From *Great Expectations*

My depression was not alleviated by the announcement, for, I had supposed that establishment to be an hotel kept by Mr Barnard, to which the Blue Boar in our town was a mere public-house. Whereas I now found Barnard to be a disembodied spirit, or a fiction, and his inn the dingiest collection of shabby buildings ever squeezed together in a rank corner as a club for Tom-cats.

We entered this haven through a wicket-gate, and were disgorged by an introductory passage into a melancholy little square that looked to me like a flat burying-ground. I thought it had the most dismal trees in it, and the most dismal sparrows, and the most dismal cats, and the most dismal houses (in number half a dozen or so), that I had ever seen. I thought the windows of the sets of chambers into which those houses were divided were in every stage of dilapidated blind and curtain, crippled flower-pot, cracked glass, dusty decay, and miserable makeshift; while To Let, To Let, To Let, glared at me from empty rooms, as if no new wretches ever came there, and the vengeance of the soul of Barnard were being slowly appeased by the gradual suicide of the present occupants and their unholy interment under the gravel. A frowzy mourning of soot and smoke attired this forlorn creation of Barnard, and it had strewn ashes on its head, and was undergoing penance and humiliation as a mere dust-hole. Thus far my sense of sight; while dry rot and wet rot and all the silent rots that rot in neglected roof and cellar, — rot of rat and mouse and bug and coaching-stables near at hand besides — addressed themselves faintly to my sense of smell, and moaned, 'Try Barnard's Mixture.'

WALK 6:
CLERKENWELL

Starting location: Holborn Circus, EC1N 2HA.

Nearest tube station: Chancery Lane or Farringdon.

Walking time: 1 hour.

Opening hours:

- MUSEUM OF THE ORDER OF ST JOHN: Monday to Saturday,
  10 a.m. to 5 p.m.; Sunday, closed.

W E BEGIN OUR WALK at Holborn Circus. The equestrian statue of Prince Albert (1874) points proudly towards Holborn Viaduct, one of the great engineering projects of Victorian London, built in the final decade of Dickens' life, between 1863 and 1869 (together with Holborn Circus itself). It may not be immediately obvious that, following Albert's gaze, you are looking at any sort of

Holborn Hill before the building of Holborn Viaduct.

bridge at all – let alone one that took five years to complete and cost
£1.5 million in Victorian currency (equivalent to at least fifty times
as much today). So walk down the slope of Charterhouse Street, and
we will explore further.

Charterhouse Street belongs to the same project. The principal
idea was to build a bridge that would span the Fleet Ditch at Holborn,
the natural valley formed by the old Fleet River, which once ran from

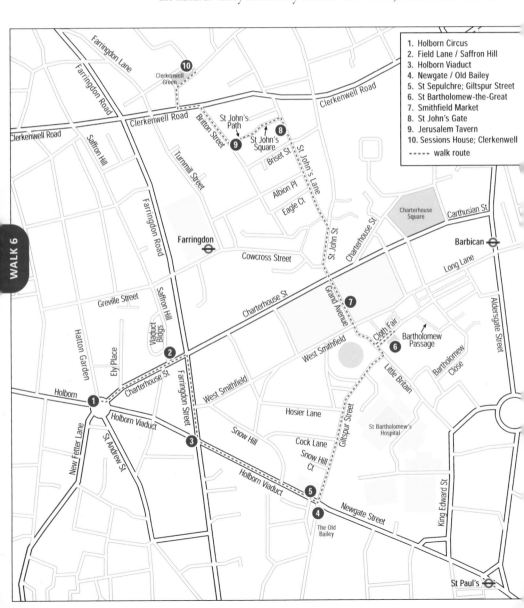

1. Holborn Circus
2. Field Lane / Saffron Hill
3. Holborn Viaduct
4. Newgate / Old Bailey
5. St Sepulchre; Giltspur Street
6. St Bartholomew-the-Great
7. Smithfield Market
8. St John's Gate
9. Jerusalem Tavern
10. Sessions House; Clerkenwell
----- walk route

WALK 6

King's Cross down to Blackfriars (the same route followed by the modern Farringdon Road). The river had long since been diverted underground, but the steep inclines that remained were a bane to horse traffic, struggling up or down Holborn Hill in wet, slippery, mud-soaked streets – the same hill, by the way, on which Dickens conjures up a fanciful 'Megalosaurus, forty feet long or so, waddling like an elephantine lizard' at the start of *Bleak House*. The Holborn scheme would also clear paths through some of London's worst slums – and Charterhouse Street was one such path.

If you walk down the street, towards the traffic lights, there is only the name of a road to evoke the district's old 'rookeries': namely the steps leading to the narrow back street of Saffron Hill, the infamous slum in *Oliver Twist*. This particular portion of Saffron Hill was actually called Field Lane and it was here that Fagin had his den. If you make a brief detour down the road, the combination of Victorian slum clearance and modern development has removed almost everything of antiquarian note. You may notice the iron-galleried flats of Viaduct Buildings on the left – London's first example of local authority housing, built by the City of London in the 1870s (after the 'model housing' already created by various charities along similar lines). One worker on the Viaduct, writing in 1869, claimed to have discovered 'all sorts of concealed passages for escape and nooks for hiding plunder in the villainous old houses of Field Lane', but one cannot help but wonder if he had read too many 'penny dreadfuls', or simply *Oliver Twist*.

Turn right at the traffic lights ahead and you will see the Viaduct itself, cast-iron girders spanning Farringdon Road at a skewed angle, its balustrade topped with statues representing 'Science' and 'Fine Art', and, on the far side, 'Commerce' and 'Agriculture'. The money was spent not simply on the bridge but on the landscaping, new roads and buildings on either side; for example, each corner of the Viaduct had an ornate Renaissance-style office block attached. If you walk under the Viaduct's girders, you will also see arched doorways, which lead to

Oliver Twist in Fagin's den, Field Lane.

WALK 6

Ornate gaslights and statuary on Holborn Viaduct.

WALK 6

Mr Squeers at the Saracen's Head, Snow Hill.

cavernous chambers underneath the bridge. These vaults have been used for shops and storage over the years and run alongside the integrated water and gas mains that were part of the original design, as well as sewers and pneumatic despatch tubes. The office blocks also incorporated staircases – one of which we can now ascend, to stand above Farringdon Road, on the Viaduct itself.

At the top, with Holborn Circus and Prince Albert behind you, keep walking along Holborn Viaduct. A little while after the bridge, you will pass Snow Hill on the left, where Nicholas Nickleby meets the foul schoolmaster Squeers at the Saracen's Head Inn. Between Snow Hill and Giltspur Street is the church of St Sepulchre-without-Newgate, opposite the Viaduct Tavern. We shall pause here a moment.

One reason to stop is a Victorian relic built into the church railings on the Giltspur Street corner: London's first public drinking fountain (as opposed to water pumps, which were used by man and beast alike), established by the Metropolitan Drinking Fountain Association in 1859. It was inaugurated by the daughter of the Archbishop of Canterbury, who took a sip of water from a silver chalice. It retains two beakers, of baser metal, on chains, and bears the legend 'Replace the Cup'.

The other point of interest – a rather grimmer one – is the Old Bailey opposite, the Central Criminal Court, atop which stands the famous golden statue of Justice. The building itself is Edwardian, but it occupies the site of Victorian London's most infamous tourist attraction. Indeed, on particular days, hundreds of the lower classes would flock from every corner of the capital to fill the nondescript junction that lies before you. Many of them arrived before dawn. If they had no food and drink, they could rely on street hawkers bustling through the crowd with snacks, such as muffins or crumpets. Gangs of teenage boys predominated, dressed in cheap fustian; many of those present were the worse for drink. The police, meanwhile, watched from the fringes but did nothing to disperse the mob. This great mass (some would argue, the very dregs of humanity) came for a 'great moral purpose' – to see a man, or woman, hanged. The site of the modern Old Bailey was once the stone fortress of Newgate prison. It was on the road beside Newgate that the scaffold was constructed, and Giltspur Street provided the best view of a hanging. Dickens himself attended a hanging and in a letter to *The Times* describes the crowds as 'thieves, low prostitutes, ruffians, and vagabonds of every kind' and writes of their antics as 'fightings, faintings, whistlings, imitations of Punch, brutal jokes, tumultuous demonstrations of indecent delight'. Dickens and others lobbied against the practice, but public execution continued until 1868. The only tangible reminder of the Newgate hangings is the clock of St Sepulchre's Church – executions invariably took place as the church's bells tolled the half-hour at 7.30 in the morning.

The first purpose-built public water fountain in London.

Continue your walk by heading down Giltspur Street, beside the church, past its octagonal watch-house (rebuilt after the Second World War, originally built to look out for body-snatching in the graveyard). Keep going, past Cock Lane (which was famous in Dickens' day for a supposed eighteenth-century haunting) and the Golden Boy statue on the corner, whose true origins and purpose, despite the plaque describing it as a memorial of the Great Fire, are not clear. When you come to the open space of West Smithfield,

The clock of St Sepulchre marked the time for Newgate hangings.

you will see a railed circular island in the middle of the square (which leads to an underground car park). Beyond it lies Smithfield Market and, immediately on your right, St Bartholomew's Hospital.

Smithfield Market, like Holborn Viaduct, was constructed in the 1860s and erased another piece of old London, which many considered as bad as the nearby slums. This was the current market's predecessor: a broad open space with temporary pens for

WALK 6

A dragon guards the entrance to Smithfield Market.

The poor-box at St Bartholomew's Hospital.

live sheep and cattle, which were driven from the countryside into the heart of the metropolis every Monday and Friday. Herds of cows would trample through the genteel suburban streets of Islington at the break of day, endangering any householders foolish enough to chance the pavement. At Smithfield itself, butchers and slaughtermen occupied the surrounding narrow lanes, where gutters ran with blood. Sikes drags Oliver Twist through old Smithfield market; and Pip turns away from it in disgust in *Great Expectations*. The old market was finally abolished in 1852 (a purpose-built market being established in Copenhagen Street in north Islington); and the current 'dead meat market' was built in high style: a Renaissance palace, whose principal thoroughfare is guarded by dragons, and topped by statues representing the great cities of the Victorian United Kingdom (London, Edinburgh, Dublin and Liverpool). The new market was opened in 1868, accompanied by a grand banquet held inside for 1,200 guests, in true Victorian fashion, for which 3,000 feet of temporary gas pipes were constructed, to light every corner. There was also a dedicated spur of railway line: the sloping ramp to the subterranean car park was once the access to the market's underground rail platforms.

St Bartholomew's Hospital (Bart's), on your right, is the oldest hospital in London, founded in 1123. If you turn right and walk past its entrance, you will also see the impressive Tudor gatehouse to the church of St Bartholomew-the-Great, founded in the same year as the hospital. Dickens makes several allusions to Bart's: Jack Hopkins in *The Pickwick Papers* appears, having just attended an accident victim at the hospital; Mrs Gamp of *Martin Chuzzlewit* mentions it in passing; the injured Cavelleto is taken there in *Little Dorrit*. Little Britain, on the far side of the hospital, is also the site of the office of Jaggers, the canny lawyer in *Great Expectations*, and his clients are said to wait for him in nearby Bartholomew Close. Both these roads are now thoroughly modern, but Cloth Fair, the road on the left of St Bartholomew's Church, still has a series of narrow alleys and quaint buildings that perhaps give a hint of old Smithfield.

The front and back of the Tudor gatehouse at St Bartholomew's Church.

If you explore St Bartholomew's Church or Cloth Fair, return to West Smithfield, turning right. Stroll through the centre of the meat market, down the aptly named Grand Avenue, whose natural light and colourful decorative ironwork give the building a cathedral-like ambience. The late-Victorian cold-storage warehouses on the far side of Charterhouse Street, to the left, are now a mix of night clubs, restaurants and office space. We shall continue straight on from the Grand Avenue, down St John Street, which was once the principal route for cattle entering the old market.

A short walk down Cowcross Street on the left would lead to Farringdon underground station, the terminus of the first underground line, which opened in 1863.

A decaying bovine sculpture on one of the warehouses on Charterhouse Street.

The cathedral-like splendour of the Grand Avenue, Smithfield Market.

St John's Gate, the sixteenth-century gatehouse that once opened on to the priory of the Knights Hospitaller.

Our journey, however, takes us further along St John Street and then down St John's Lane on the left. At the end of the lane is a remarkable survival, albeit much restored: St John's Gate, a sixteenth-century gatehouse that once opened on to the priory of the Knights Hospitaller. The priory was dissolved under Henry VIII, and the building has had various uses in the succeeding centuries. Samuel Johnson worked here, and Dickens knew it as a public house and meeting room, called the Jerusalem Tavern, where he attended meetings of the Urban Club, a literary society which held annual suppers celebrating Shakespeare's birthday.

Go through St John's Gate and turn left down the alley called St John's Path. This will bring you to Britton Street, next to the modern Jerusalem Tavern. The interior resembles an old pub, and the building dates from the eighteenth century, but appearances are a little deceptive – it has been licensed only since 1996. Street directories from the period reveal that the property was a watchmaker's shop in the Victorian era – a profession for which Clerkenwell was then famous.

Turn right from St John's Path, then left down Clerkenwell Road. Cross over and turn right into the open expanse of Clerkenwell Green. Originally a village green, it was paved by the eighteenth century, and in the nineteenth was a meeting place for the Chartists and supporters of Irish home rule – a radical tradition continued by the presence of the Marx Memorial Library at No. 37, a building that Dickens would have known as a charity school.

The heart of the Green retains twentieth-century red telephone boxes and an easily overlooked Victorian survivor: a concrete cattle trough, now a planter for flowers, provided by the Metropolitan Drinking Fountain and Cattle Trough

The Jerusalem Tavern was a watchmaker's shop in the Victorian era.

Assocation, a later version of the body that erected the Giltspur Street fountain (many of these survive throughout London). On the western side of the Green is the old Middlesex Sessions House, built in 1780, once the largest courthouse in England, now owned by the Freemasons. The district of Middlesex covered all of north London, excluding the City of London, and sundry rural areas. Criminals would be brought here for the quarter sessions – sets of hearings convened four times each year, to hear charges that could not be dealt with summarily by a justice of the peace. Clerkenwell Green is where Oliver Twist is accused of robbing Mr Brownlow. Mr Bumble also tells Mrs Mann that his trip to London will involve a 'matter before the quarter-sessions at Clerkinwell'.

WALK 6

The Marx Memorial Library, formerly a schoolhouse, on Clerkenwell Green.

A view of Clerkenwell Green in the eighteenth century.

The district of Clerkenwell contains other Dickens assocations: the banker Mr Lorry in *A Tale of Two Cities* has his abode nearby, and likewise the taxidermist Mr Venus of *Our Mutual Friend*, though neither location is precisely specified. The attempted robbery of 'the old cove at the book-stall' has a more specific association with this spot. From the Green, Oliver is pursued by a mob:

The tradesman leaves his counter, and the car-man his waggon; the butcher throws down his tray; the baker his basket; the milkman his pail; the errand-boy his parcels; the school-boy his marbles ... they run, pell-mell, helter-skelter, slap-dash: tearing, yelling, screaming, knocking down the passengers as they turn the corners, rousing up the dogs, and astonishing the fowls: and streets, squares, and courts, re-echo with the sound.

We do not know precisely where Oliver ran, and so you may choose any street to make your exit and finish your walk – hopefully, with no-one in pursuit.

Left: Oliver Twist sees the Artful Dodger rob Mr Brownlow at a bookshop on Clerkenwell Green.

Opposite bottom: The old Sessions House on Clerkenwell Green.

WALK 6

A water trough provided by the Metropolitan Drinking Fountain and Cattle Trough Assocation.

THE CONDEMNED MAN AT NEWGATE
From 'A Visit to Newgate' in *Sketches by Boz*

WALK 6

We entered the first cell. It was a stone dungeon, eight feet long by six wide, with a bench at the upper end, under which were a common rug, a bible, and prayer-book. An iron candlestick was fixed into the wall at the side; and a small high window in the back admitted as much air and light as could struggle in between a double row of heavy, crossed iron bars. It contained no other furniture of any description.

Conceive the situation of a man, spending his last night on earth in this cell. Buoyed up with some vague and undefined hope of reprieve, he knew not why — indulging in some wild and visionary idea of escaping, he knew not how — hour after hour of the three preceding days allowed him for preparation, has fled with a speed which no man living would deem possible, for none but this dying man can know. He has wearied his friends with entreaties, exhausted the attendants with importunities, neglected in his feverish restlessness the timely warnings of his spiritual consoler; and, now that the illusion is at last dispelled, now that eternity is before him and guilt behind, now that his fears of death amount almost to madness, and an overwhelming sense of his helpless, hopeless state rushes upon him, he is lost and stupefied, and has neither thoughts to turn to, nor power to call upon, the Almighty Being, from whom alone he can seek mercy and forgiveness, and before whom his repentance can alone avail.

Hours have glided by, and still he sits upon the same stone bench with folded arms, heedless alike of the fast decreasing time before him, and the urgent entreaties of the good man at his side. The feeble light is wasting gradually, and the deathlike stillness of the street without, broken only by the rumbling of some passing vehicle which echoes mournfully through the empty yards, warns him that the night is waning fast away. The deep bell of St Paul's strikes — one! He heard it; it has roused him. Seven hours left! He paces the narrow limits of his cell with rapid strides, cold drops of terror starting on his forehead, and every muscle of his frame quivering with agony. Seven hours! He suffers himself to be led to his seat, mechanically takes the bible which is placed in his hand, and tries to read and listen.

No: his thoughts will wander. The book is torn and soiled by use — and like the book he read his lessons in, at school, just forty years ago! He has never bestowed a thought upon it, perhaps, since he left it as a child: and yet the place, the time, the room — nay, the very boys he played with, crowd as vividly before him as if they were scenes of yesterday; and some forgotten phrase, some childish word, rings in his ears like the echo of one uttered but a minute since. The voice of the clergyman recalls him to himself. He is reading from the sacred book its solemn promises of pardon for repentance, and its awful denunciation of obdurate men. He falls upon his knees and clasps his hands to pray. Hush! what sound was that? He starts upon his feet. It cannot be two yet. Hark! Two quarters have struck; — the third — the fourth. It is! Six hours left. Tell him not of repentance! Six hours' repentance for eight times six years of guilt and sin! He buries his face in his hands, and throws himself on the bench.

Worn with watching and excitement, he sleeps, and the same unsettled state of mind pursues him in his dreams. An insupportable load is taken from his breast; he is walking with his wife in a pleasant field, with the bright sky above them, and a fresh and boundless prospect on every side — how different from the stone walls of Newgate! She is looking — not as she did when he saw her for the last time in that dreadful place, but as she used when he loved her — long, long ago, before misery and ill-treatment had altered her looks, and vice had changed his nature, and she is leaning upon his arm, and looking up into his face with tenderness and affection — and he does NOT strike her now, nor rudely shake her from him. And oh! how glad he is to tell her all he had forgotten in that last hurried interview, and to fall on his knees before her and fervently beseech her pardon for all the unkindness and cruelty that wasted her form and broke her heart! The scene suddenly changes. He is on his trial again: there are the judge and jury, and prosecutors, and witnesses, just as they were

The condemned man's cell at Newgate prison.

WALK 6

before. How full the court is — what a sea of heads — with a gallows, too, and a scaffold — and how all those people stare at HIM! Verdict, 'Guilty.' No matter; he will escape.

The night is dark and cold, the gates have been left open, and in an instant he is in the street, flying from the scene of his imprisonment like the wind. The streets are cleared, the open fields are gained and the broad, wide country lies before him. Onward he dashes in the midst of darkness, over hedge and ditch, through mud and pool, bounding from spot to spot with a speed and lightness, astonishing even to himself. At length he pauses; he must be safe from pursuit now; he will stretch himself on that bank and sleep till sunrise.

A period of unconsciousness succeeds. He wakes, cold and wretched. The dull, gray light of morning is stealing into the cell, and falls upon the form of the attendant turnkey. Confused by his dreams, he starts from his uneasy bed in momentary uncertainty. It is but momentary. Every object in the narrow cell is too frightfully real to admit of doubt or mistake. He is the condemned felon again, guilty and despairing; and in two hours more will be dead.

WALK 7:
ST PAUL'S AND BOROUGH

Starting location: St Martin's-le-Grand, EC1A 4EN.

Nearest tube station: St Paul's.

Walking time: 1½ hours.

Opening hours:

- ST PAUL'S CATHEDRAL: open for sightseeing Monday to Saturday, 8.30 a.m. to 4 p.m.; on Sundays open for worship only.
- BOROUGH MARKET: Thursday, 11 a.m. to 5 p.m.; Friday, 12 noon to 6 p.m.; Saturday, 8 a.m. to 5 p.m.; Sunday to Wednesday, closed.
- OLD OPERATING THEATRE: daily, 10.30 a.m. to 5 p.m.

WE BEGIN OUR WALK at the exit to St Paul's underground station, on the corner of St Martin's-le-Grand. Victorians flocked down this road, but not just tourists on the way to St Paul's Cathedral: this was the site of the General Post Office, a massive classical building, constructed in 1825–9. The rush for the final six o'clock post inside the great hall, the nightly departure of dozens of mail-coaches speeding in all directions, the glow of the thousand flaring gaslights that lit the building's façade – all this was a famous spectacle of the Victorian metropolis. Needless to say, Dickens knew this spot very well: the newlywed Browdies and Miss Squeers stop here in *Nicholas Nickleby*; Anthony Chuzzlewit's firm in *Martin Chuzzlewit* is somewhere nearby; likewise, the hotel at which John Jasper stays in *Edwin Drood*; and Cavaletto in *Little Dorrit* is hit by a speeding mail-coach in Aldersgate, immediately to the north ('They come a racing out of Lad Lane and Wood Street at twelve or fourteen mile an hour, them Mails do. The only wonder is, that people ain't killed oftener …').

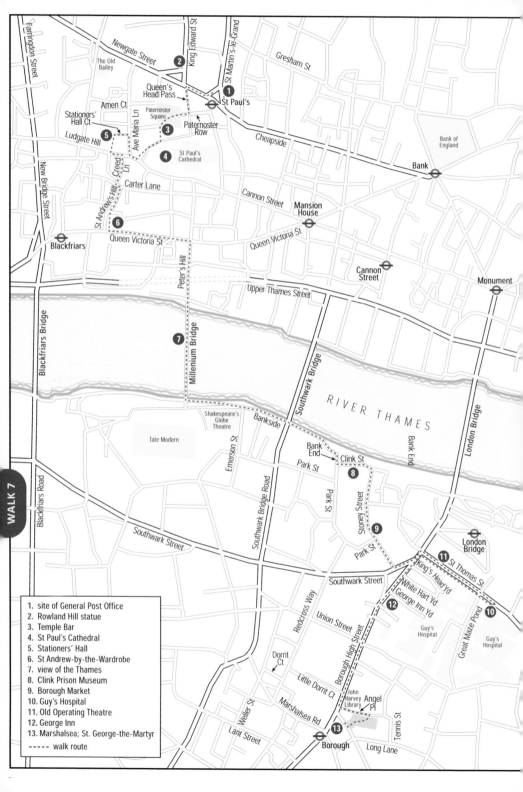

1. site of General Post Office
2. Rowland Hill statue
3. Temple Bar
4. St Paul's Cathedral
5. Stationers' Hall
6. St Andrew-by-the-Wardrobe
7. view of the Thames
8. Clink Prison Museum
9. Borough Market
10. Guy's Hospital
11. Old Operating Theatre
12. George Inn
13. Marshalsea; St. George-the-Martyr
- - - - - walk route

The Post Office at
St Martin's-le-Grand
(right, built 1825–9).

From the corner of St Martin's-le-Grand, walk along Newgate Street to nearby King Edward Street. You will see the garden of Christ Church Greyfriars, also known as Christ Church Newgate, in the ruins of the church, destroyed during the Second World War. A little way down King Edward Street you will see a statue of Rowland Hill, the founder of the Penny Post – the standard, universal charge for postage which, combined with the use of pre-paid adhesive stamps, created the modern postal system in 1840 (he stands outside an Edwardian Post Office building). We shall, however, turn left, down Queen's Head Passage on the opposite side of Newgate Street from King Edward Street.

This pedestrianised lane leads us into the modern development of Paternoster Square, which replaces an old part of London once famous for its bookshops and publishers, but utterly levelled by bombing in the Second World War. Take the first right on to Paternoster Row and you will come to the

Statue of Rowland Hill,
founder of the modern
Post Office.

WALK 7

square itself. The central column, although it might be taken for a miniature of the Monument to the Great Fire of London, is a 2003 tribute to the destruction of the bookshops of Paternoster Row during the Blitz. There is, however, an unusual antique piece of old London in the square, albeit slightly misplaced from its original location: the arched gateway that leads through to St Paul's is Temple Bar, which stood on Fleet Street until the 1870s. Temple Bar was designed by Wren in the 1670s (replacing an earlier gate) and marked the western boundary of the City of London, where, traditionally, the monarch – if venturing into the City – would observe the ritual of stopping to seek the Lord Mayor's permission to enter. It was on this gateway that grisly displays of traitors' bodies were made for the edification of the public. It was removed from Fleet Street in 1878, having long been infamous as an obstruction on that busy thoroughfare, and in 1880 was bought by the brewer Henry Meux to grace his Hertfordshire estate. It was restored to the City of London by the Temple Bar Trust in 2004, though on a site where it can never again impede traffic.

Wren's arch now provides access to his masterpiece, St Paul's Cathedral, built between 1675 and 1710. The shadow of the cathedral

Temple Bar stood on Fleet Street until dismantled in 1878. It was returned to London in 2004.

falls upon many of Dickens' novels: from simple tourism (the Browdies come to see it in *Nicholas Nickleby*; David Copperfield takes Peggotty to its summit while doing the London sights) to more evocative scenes, such as when the wretched crossing-sweeper Jo sees the cross atop the dome, 'so golden, so high up, so far out of his reach' – a metaphor of his own hopeless condition. The cathedral itself is little changed and well worth a visit – particularly if you are willing to ascend to the galleries. Its environs, on the other hand, like Paternoster Square, suffered greatly during the Blitz: there is little in St Paul's Churchyard and

St Paul's Cathedral, seen from the east.

surrounding streets that Dickens might recognise. If we venture a little further afield, however, there are occasional reminders of the numerous small courtyards and narrow lanes that once filled this ancient part of London.

From the front steps of the cathedral, head down Ludgate Hill in search of one such courtyard. Turn right down Ave Maria Lane and then left into Stationers' Hall Court. This is the home of the Stationers' Company, an ancient guild of the City of London, which once held a monopoly on printing, and the responsibility to check and register all books produced in England.

Stationers' Hall, near St Paul's. The Stationers are one of the ancient guilds of the City of London.

The livery hall itself dates back to 1673. Amen Court, a private road further up Ave Maria Lane, also contains houses of a similar age, reserved for canons of the cathedral.

Leave Stationers' Hall Court by the alley on the south side, and it will bring you back to Ludgate Hill. Turn left, and go down Creed Lane on the far side of the road, turning left on to Carter Lane, then take a swift right down St Andrew's Hill. This will lead you to St Andrew-by-the-Wardrobe, Wren's last City church, finished in 1695 (rebuilt after the Second World War), with

WALK 7

The alley around St Andrew-by-the-Wardrobe.

the rectory house beside it dating from 1766. Like the Stationers' Hall, the church has no specific association with Dickens, but the claustrophobic alley of Wardrobe Terrace that runs around its boundary gives some flavour of how the district might have appeared in the Victorian period. A little to the west of here stood Printing House Square, the original home of *The Times* newspaper, where the daily despatch of heavy bundles of papers to dozens of newspaper boys was another tourist favourite, similar to the departure of mail-coaches at St Martin's-le-Grand.

Leave St Andrew's by descending to Queen Victoria Street at the far side of the church, and turn left. The large Edwardian Faraday Building, next door but one from the church, was originally the Post Office's first London telephone exchange, opened in 1902. It was built on the site of Doctors' Commons, the complex of small law courts in which Dickens began his journalistic career as a shorthand reporter. Steerforth in *David Copperfield* describes Doctors' Commons as 'a lazy old nook near St Paul's Churchyard … a little out-of-the-way place, where they administer what is called ecclesiastical law, and play all kinds of tricks with obsolete old monsters of acts of Parliament'. In appearance, Doctors' Commons was a close cousin to the Inns of Chancery, such as Staple Inn and Clifford's Inn (see Walk 5). Jingle obtains a marriage licence from Doctors' Commons in *The Pickwick Papers* (special marriage licences from the Commons were a necessity for hastily arranged alliances in Victorian fact and fiction); and the lawyers Spenlow and Jorkins in *David Copperfield* are also based here.

Continue along Queen Victoria Street, past the impressive gates of the College of Arms on your left (added to the building in 1956, taken from Goodrich Court, Herefordshire), and turn right down Peter's Hill, towards the Millenium Bridge. We are heading south of the river.

The bridge, closed for two years soon after its opening because of an unexpected wobble generated by tourists' footsteps, offers a unique view of the cathedral and the river Thames. The view of the cathedral is a modern perspective: there was no bridge here in Dickens' time, only riverside factories, warehouses and wharves, on both sides of the river. Nonetheless, this part of the river features in his fiction. Facing Blackfriars Bridge (with the cathedral behind you, looking right), you will see the general location of Murdstone & Grimby's wine and spirit warehouse in *David Copperfield*, which lay somewhere hereabouts – a transposition of the blacking

Perusing legal records at Doctors' Commons.

warehouse at Hungerford Bridge (the next bridge upstream), where Dickens himself was obliged to work as a boy. Jo, the crossing-sweeper from *Bleak House*, rests on Blackfriars Bridge (albeit an earlier version, the present bridge having been built in the 1860s); Mr George crosses the bridge in *Bleak House*; and Pip in *Great Expectations* practises his rowing here on the river, training himself up to spirit away the convict Magwitch along the Thames.

Cross the bridge. The south side of the river brings you to a modern tourist trail that encompasses Tate Modern (the modern art gallery, formerly a 1940s power station) and the replica of

WALK 7

A Victorian view of St Paul's, where the modern Millennium Bridge crosses the river.

The typical mid-Victorian iron and glass roof of Borough Market.

Shakespeare's Globe (opened in 1997). Turn left towards the Globe and walk along the river. Dickens would perhaps have recognised No. 49 Bankside (built *c.* 1710) in the row of houses just before the theatre – but not necessarily as the home of Sir Christopher Wren, as a plaque proudly proclaims. The local tradition that Wren watched the building of his cathedral from this spot referred to a specific long-demolished building nearby, its history appropriated by a later owner of No. 49.

After the Globe Theatre comes Southwark Bridge, a rather fanciful Edwardian creation. The previous version of this bridge features heavily in *Little Dorrit*; and the river scavengers, Gaffer and Lizzie Hexam, row past this stretch of the river in *Our Mutual Friend.*

Keep going under the bridge along the Thames path and, at the Anchor public house, follow the road as it goes under the archway between Victorian warehouses at Clink Street. The Clink Prison Museum celebrates the jail that once stood on this site, burnt down during the Gordon Riots of 1780. The Riots also form the backdrop to Dickens' historical novel *Barnaby Rudge* and he mentions the prison:

> *In two hours, six-and-thirty fires were raging – six-and-thirty great conflagrations: among them the Borough Clink in Tooley Street, the King's Bench, the Fleet, and the New Bridewell … in every quarter the muskets of the troops were heard above the shouts and tumult of the mob…*

Turn right up Stoney Street, and keep going until you come to the Market Porter pub on your right, and Borough Market on your left. The market is open on Thursdays to Saturdays only, and if you come at another time, when there are no stalls, you may be unimpressed. It sits within a dingy set of odd little streets and spaces beneath the railway arches that lead to nearby London Bridge station. The principal market buildings, opposite the Market Porter pub, were built in the 1850s and 1860s, in the typical iron and glass style that the Victorians favoured. Dickens mentions the street market that predated these 1850s buildings in *The Pickwick Papers*.

At the end of Stoney Street, we shall take a brief detour into medical London. Turn left and go round the corner on to Borough High Street. Cross the road and go down St Thomas Street. This street once contained two hospitals, which would have been well known to Dickens: Guy's and St Thomas's. On the right, after Great Maze Pond (actually a street name), Guy's Hospital remains, with gates and courtyard dating to the 1720s. In *Martin Chuzzlewit*, we learn in passing that the husband of Mrs Gamp died here. On the opposite side of the road, St Thomas's has vanished – it moved to Lambeth in the 1860s, selling the land to the railway for expanding London Bridge station. Yet one of London's most unusual museums is a reminder of its presence, namely the old operating theatre in the garret of St Thomas's Church. Some of the wings of the hospital were built around the church, and the garret seems to have been a convenient space to build a theatre, allowing

The coat of arms of Guy's Hospital.

A late-Victorian photograph of Guy's Hospital.

WALK 7

The herb garret at the Old Operating Theatre Museum.

The nurse Mrs Gamp (right).

WALK 7

medical students a separate entrance to come and watch surgery – all performed without anaesthetic.

Walk back up St Thomas Street to Borough High Street and turn left. On your left, you will pass a series of odd enclosed little roads: King's Head Yard, White Hart Yard, George Inn Yard, Queen's Head Yard, and others. These yards mark the sites of the numerous coaching inns for which the Borough was once famous, before the coming of the railways. Sam Weller of *The Pickwick Papers* makes his appearance at the White Hart and there is a passing mention of the George Inn, where Sam walks by, 'awakening all the echoes in George Yard ... with several chaste and extremely correct imitations of a drover's whistle, delivered in a tone of peculiar richness and volume'. These old inns were at their peak in Dickens' youth, but the arrival of the steam locomotive marked their gradual doom. A substantial portion of the George Inn still survives, so do take a walk down George Yard. Elsewhere, the only clue is a few incongruous old timbers or a cobbled courtyard.

Having passed the coaching inn, we move from the jollity of Pickwick to a more sombre work. Past the old mid-Victorian rooftop street sign for the 'Monster Ready Made Bespoke Clothing Establishment' (just after Union Street, on the left) we approach the site of the Marshalsea – the debtors' prison that features in *Little Dorrit*, and in which Dickens' own father, John, was himself imprisoned, to his son's eternal

A mid-Victorian painted sign for 'The Monster Ready Made & Bespoke Clothing Establishment'.

shame – a fact not revealed to the public until after the author's death. Look for the John Harvard Library on the left. The narrow path beside it is Angel Place. The long brick wall on the right is believed to be the southern boundary of the old prison. Dickens, unlike Little Amy Dorrit, did not lodge inside the prison but in Lant Street (a little further down Borough High Street, on the right; nothing from Dickens' time survives there). Nonetheless, if you walk through the iron gates into the old churchyard beyond, now a public garden, its walls lined with gravestones, you are crossing the same threshold that was crossed not only by William Dorrit, but by John Dickens and by the young novelist himself, when visiting his father.

Once you have passed through the gate, you will also see St George the Martyr, the church in which Amy Dorrit was christened and, at the novel's climax, married. For a distinctly unassuming character, she has

WALK 7

The lanes and alleys off Borough High Street once led to the yards of coaching inns.

Little Dorrit is married
to Arthur Clenham at
St George-the-Martyr.

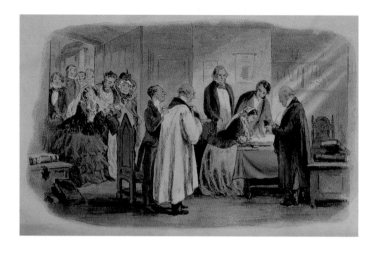

WALK 7

left her mark in the area – there is a small 'Little Dorrit' in the stained glass at the east end of the church, as well as a Dorrit Street, Dorrit Court, and Little Dorrit Court on the opposite side of the High Street. Indeed, the Borough is rather proud of Dickens. Lant Street – the site of his lodgings during his father's imprisonment, and also of Bob Sawyer's in *The Pickwick Papers* – has had a Charles Dickens School since 1911. There are also plans for a Dickens monument in the piazza between the Marshalsea wall and St George's Church. Whether Dickens would welcome being memorialised at the very site of his childhood humiliation is a matter of conjecture.

A rockery of tombstones
in the churchyard of
St George-the-Martyr.

FOCUS ON: *THE BOROUGH*

The Tabard Inn in Borough High Street is the starting point for the pilgrims of Chaucer's *Canterbury Tales* and many of Borough High Street's coaching inns could lay claim to several hundred years of history when Dickens began *The Pickwick Papers* in 1836. The wanderings of the Pickwickians, however, represent the high watermark of the coaching network, which would swiftly be rendered obsolete by the appearance of the railways – not least nearby London Bridge Station, which opened in 1836 and was subsequently rebuilt, enlarged and altered several times in the following decades, a series of changes that created the sprawling and confused structure we know today. The station, with its lofty viaduct, would cast a gloomy shadow over the whole district. When those viaducts extended westwards to connect with the new Charing Cross station in the 1860s, Borough Market became part of a miserable labyrinth, huddled beneath the roar of the passing steam engines.

In truth, Pickwick's Borough was not how many Londoners pictured the district. The coaching inns were a quaint oasis among poverty and crime. One campaigning booklet from the 1850s describes 'The Mint', opposite St George's Church:

> Its evil character has not departed from it. With a gin-shop at the High-street end, and St George's Workhouse at the other, it has on either side of it congeries of filthy courts unfit for habitation. The houses are tumbling down, the approaches in a miserable condition … Let us take one of the courts on the south side of it: Wallis's-alley, where the houses (of wood) are in the most distressing state of dilapidation: the ceilings have fallen, the floors are full of holes, and the windows glassless.

It is hard to judge the degree of criminality in the Borough, as opposed to any other poor district in London, but a letter to *The Times* in the 1860s describes it as 'pre-eminently abundant' with garotters (muggers) and 'the lowest of the low class of beer-shops in London, and probably in the world, the acknowledged haunts of burglars, thieves and forgers'. Forgery was a local speciality. A quick glance at court reports for 1836, the year of *Pickwick*, soon finds a William Withers, auctioneer, charged with possession of

'17 sixpences washed with the colour of gold, with intent to utter the same as half-sovereigns'. He is given into custody by a 'girl of the town', of the Borough Road, whose landlady he has paid in false coin.

The presence of three prisons in the area did nothing to enhance its reputation. The site of King's Bench (later called Queen's Bench, during Victoria's reign; demolished 1880) is now a council estate between Great Suffolk Street and Borough Road. This was a prison reserved mainly for debtors despatched by the King's Bench court, but also for 'contempt, libel, and misdemeanour'. In the early years of Victoria's reign it was still possible to pay a premium to reside outside the prison walls within the 'Rules' ('the whole of St George's Fields, one side of Blackman Street, and part of High Street in the Borough'), like the penurious Brays in *Nicholas Nickleby*, whose daughter Ralph Nickleby schemes to have married to the miserable Arthur Gride. Only a hundred yards distant from the 'Bench' lay Horsemonger Lane Gaol (also demolished in 1880; now gardens behind the Inner London Crown Court on Newington Causeway) for 'felons and debtors'. Murderers might be hanged at Horsemonger Lane, as well as at Newgate, and it provided a somewhat superior spectacle: the condemned were hanged from a scaffold specially erected on the prison's roof.

Last, of course, there was the Marshalsea. Interestingly, Mr Rugg, the lawyer in *Little Dorrit*, recommends that Arthur Clenham choose to be arrested for a debt that might get him sent to the King's Bench, rather than the Marshalsea: 'Now, you know what the Marshalsea is. Very close. Excessively confined...' Once Arthur is in the Marshalsea, he presses him again: 'This is an extensive affair of yours; and your remaining here where a man can come for a pound or two, is remarked upon as not in keeping.' Dickens is mocking the idea of any gradations of 'respectability' in debt; and it is Arthur's fond memories of Amy Dorrit that tie him to the prison. Did the author himself have some perverse fondness for the site of his father's confinement? There was certainly stigma and shame attached to it, yet his biographer would write:

They had no want of bodily comforts there. His father's income, still going on, was amply sufficient for that; and in every respect indeed but elbow-room, I have heard him say, the family lived more

comfortably in prison than they had done for a long time out of it.
They were waited on still by the maid-of-all-work from Bayham
Street, the orphan girl of the Chatham workhouse, from whose sharp
little worldly and also kindly ways he took his first impression of
the Marchioness in the Old Curiosity Shop ... Besides breakfast, he
had supper also in the prison, and got to his lodging generally at
nine o'clock. The gates closed always at ten.

The Marshalsea closed in 1842, with the buildings themselves
demolished shortly after Dickens' death. Yet the great author's
memories have assured the Marshalsea a certain sort of immortality.

THE WHITE HART COACHING INN
From *The Pickwick Papers*

In the Borough especially, there still remain some half-dozen old inns,
which have preserved their external features unchanged, and which have
escaped alike the rage for public improvement and the encroachments of
private speculation. Great, rambling queer old places they are, with
galleries, and passages, and staircases, wide enough and antiquated enough
to furnish materials for a hundred ghost stories, supposing we should ever
be reduced to the lamentable necessity of inventing any, and that the world
should exist long enough to exhaust the innumerable veracious legends
connected with old London Bridge, and its adjacent neighbourhood on the
Surrey side.

It was in the yard of one of these inns – of no less celebrated a one than
the White Hart – that a man was busily employed in brushing the dirt off
a pair of boots, early on the morning succeeding the events narrated in the
last chapter. He was habited in a coarse, striped waistcoat, with black calico
sleeves, and blue glass buttons; drab breeches and leggings. A bright red
handkerchief was wound in a very loose and unstudied style round his neck,
and an old white hat was carelessly thrown on one side of his head. There
were two rows of boots before him, one cleaned and the other dirty, and at

WALK 7

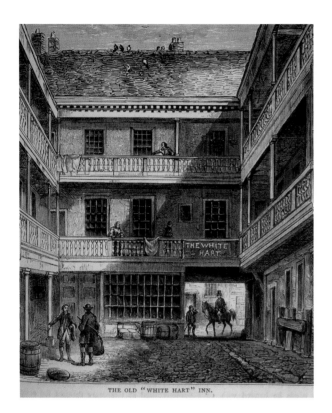

THE OLD "WHITE HART" INN.

every addition he made to the clean row, he paused from his work, and contemplated its results with evident satisfaction.

The yard presented none of that bustle and activity which are the usual characteristics of a large coach inn. Three or four lumbering wagons, each with a pile of goods beneath its ample canopy, about the height of the second-floor window of an ordinary house, were stowed away beneath a lofty roof which extended over one end of the yard; and another, which was probably to commence its journey that morning, was drawn out into the open space. A double tier of bedroom galleries, with old clumsy balustrades, ran round

WALK 7

Borough contained a number of galleried coaching inns, including the White Hart, featured in *The Pickwick Papers*.

two sides of the straggling area, and a double row of bells to correspond, sheltered from the weather by a little sloping roof, hung over the door leading to the bar and coffee-room. Two or three gigs and chaise-carts were wheeled up under different little sheds and pent-houses; and the occasional heavy tread of a cart-horse, or rattling of a chain at the farther end of the yard, announced to anybody who cared about the matter, that the stable lay in that direction. When we add that a few boys in smock-frocks were lying asleep on heavy packages, wool-packs, and other articles that were scattered about on heaps of straw, we have described as fully as need be the general appearance of the yard of the White Hart Inn, High Street, Borough, on the particular morning in question.

A loud ringing of one of the bells was followed by the appearance of a smart chambermaid in the upper sleeping gallery, who, after tapping at one of the doors, and receiving a request from within, called over the balustrades – 'Sam!'

WALK 8:
CITY AND RIVERSIDE

Tip: A weekday lunchtime will give you full access to churches, the Royal Exchange and the Cornhill chop-houses – but this walk can be enjoyed on any day of the week.

Starting location: One New Change, EC4M 9AF.

Nearest tube station: St Paul's.

Walking time: 2 hours (3½ hours if following the riverside extension).

Opening hours:

- ST MARY-LE-BOW CHURCH: Monday to Wednesday, 7.30 a.m. to 6 p.m.; Thursday, 7.30 a.m. to 6.30 p.m.; Friday, 7.30 a.m. to 4 p.m.; Saturday and Sunday, closed.
- BANK OF ENGLAND MUSEUM: Monday to Friday, 10 a.m. to 5 p.m.; Saturday and Sunday, closed.
- ROYAL EXCHANGE: Monday to Friday, 10 a.m. to 6 p.m. (shops); 8 a.m. to 11 p.m. (cafés, restaurants); Saturday and Sunday, closed.
- SIMPSON'S CHOP-HOUSE: Monday to Friday, 11.30 a.m. to 3.30 p.m.; Saturday and Sunday, closed.
- GEORGE AND VULTURE CHOP-HOUSE: Monday to Friday, 12 noon to 2.30 p.m.; Saturday and Sunday, closed.
- MONUMENT: daily, 9.30 a.m. to 5.30 p.m.
- ST. OLAVE'S CHURCH: Monday to Friday, 9 a.m. to 5 p.m.; Saturday and Sunday, closed.
- DOCKLANDS MUSEUM: daily, 10 a.m. to 6 p.m.

IT MAY SEEM a peculiar decision to begin a Dickens walk at a modern shopping centre, but if you take the lift at the One New Change centre, you can ascend to a sixth-floor viewing gallery, with a majestic view of St Paul's Cathedral and the western portion of the City of London.

To picture this view in Dickens' day, you must strip away the skyscrapers and tall office blocks. Imagine a low-level metropolis where the cathedral is supreme, albeit blackened by the soot of thousands of chimneys, where the smoke-stacks of breweries and factories line the south bank of the Thames, and the river is filled with sailing ships, steamboats and coal barges. Look, in particular, for the spires of the capital's churches – these were the landmarks that towered above the bustling streets. The sound of the city was different, too, of course: not the hum and roar of car engines, but the rattle of iron-shod wheels, punctuated by the cries of peripetatic street sellers and the regular peal of bells.

Leave One New Change by the exit directly facing the cathedral. Turn right from the centre, and right again down Cheapside. This was once one of the great working thoroughfares of the Victorian metropolis, inhabited by harried clerks and businessmen, and 'men's shops: hosiers and shirtmakers, tailors and tobacconists, and above all by jewellers'. The stagecoach taking Pip of *Great Expectations* to London comes to a coaching inn just off Cheapside. The street now postdates Dickens, although St Mary-le-Bow remains – built by Wren and rebuilt

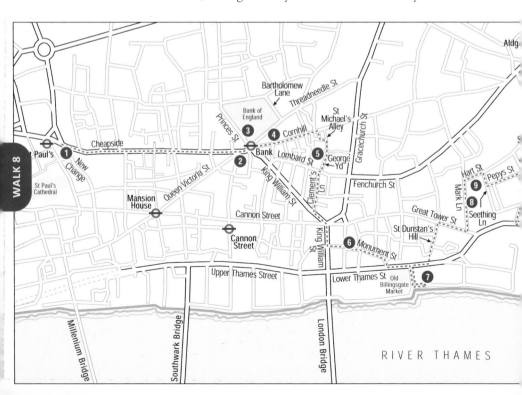

after the Second World War. Traditionally, only those who live within the sound of its church bells are truly entitled to be called Cockneys.

Continue down Cheapside until you reach the great junction that contains the Mansion House, the Royal Exchange and the Bank of England. The Mansion House is on the right, on the far side of Queen Victoria Street, a permanent residence for the Lord Mayor of the City of London, completed in 1758. It is a magnificent Palladian building, now a little dwarfed by its surroundings, designed to be fit for the office of the Lord Mayor, not least accommodating his annual round of grand balls and prodigious banquets. The Mansion House also contained a 'police court' (magistrates' court) over which the Lord Mayor presided – it is here that Kit is taken in *The Old Curiosity Shop*, following his arrest on bogus charges.

The Bank of England stands on the left, between Princes Street and Threadneedle Street. The Bank's tall windowless boundary wall dates from the 1820s, but the buildings behind it were built in the 1920s and 1930s. It does, however, contain a small museum accessible from its far side on Bartholomew Lane, which includes an eighteenth-century office and displays of currency through the ages.

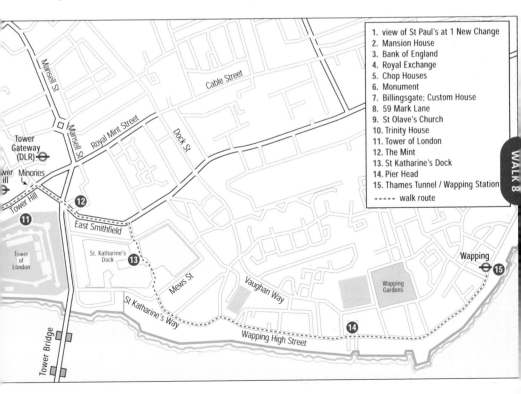

1. view of St Paul's at 1 New Change
2. Mansion House
3. Bank of England
4. Royal Exchange
5. Chop Houses
6. Monument
7. Billingsgate; Custom House
8. 59 Mark Lane
9. St Olave's Church
10. Trinity House
11. Tower of London
12. The Mint
13. St Katharine's Dock
14. Pier Head
15. Thames Tunnel / Wapping Station
----- walk route

WALK 8

The Lord Mayor's Mansion House (opened 1758).

Cross the junction to the Royal Exchange, with its grand Corinthian façade. The Exchange was opened in 1844, replacing a 1660s building that had been destroyed by fire in 1838. It served as a centre of commerce for merchants and City businessmen – with a central trading floor and surrounding offices – until 1939. It is now an upmarket shopping centre in the heart of the City. The equestrian statue that dominates the front of the Exchange is an 1844 tribute to the Duke of Wellington, the great military leader who was still prominent, late in his life, as an elder statesman. The Exchange does not figure much in Dickens' work but receives numerous passing mentions in *Dombey and Son*, whose City offices, we are told, are not too far distant. If you visit the Exchange on a weekday, do wander inside and admire the interior.

A late-Victorian photograph of the Bank of England.

Carry on your walk down Cornhill, on the right-hand side of the Exchange. This was one of the great mercantile avenues of the City and is mentioned several times in Dickens' work: Freeman's Court, a road

WALK 8

The interior of the Royal Exchange (opened 1844).

demolished during the building of the Royal Exchange, contains the offices of the lawyers Dodson and Fogg in *The Pickwick Papers*; the benificent Cheerybles' office in *Nicholas Nickleby* is somewhere in this area; likewise that of their antithesis, Scrooge in *A Christmas Carol*. The older buildings hereabouts are now largely Edwardian, but there are two interesting Victorian survivals in the maze of little alleys on the right-hand side of Cornhill, namely two 'chop-houses' – Simpson's (in Ball Court), and the George and Vulture (in St Michael's Alley). Turn down Ball Court and you will find Simpson's. Continue down the white, covered alley past Simpson's, and take a left when you emerge into Castle Court. The George and Vulture will be on your right, with its entrance in St Michael's Alleyon the right.

The City shop of Solomon Gills, in *Dombey and Son*.

Chop-houses were the lunchtime restaurant of choice for Victorian City clerks, typically partitioned into curtained-off wooden booths, specialising in quickly prepared, sizzling chops and steaks. The George and Vulture takes it name from the coaching inn that once stood in its immediate

WALK 8

Inside a typical Victorian office, belonging to the Cheerybles in *Nicholas Nickleby*.

Simpson's chop-house, off Cornhill.

vicinity, the residence of Mr Pickwick for many of the London chapters of *The Pickwick Papers*. Charles Dickens Junior, writing in 1892, recalled the original inn and noted that it was 'pulled down quite a long while ago'. Nonetheless, its successor still provides a meeting place for ardent 'Pickwickians'.

Escape the alleys by going straight past the George and Vulture's door and into George Yard, then straight on to Lombard Street. It was here that the young Dickens, aged only seventeen in 1829, engaged in a doomed romance with Maria Beadnell, the daughter of a banker, who lived at No. 2, next to her father's business. It was a semi-clandestine courtship, which petered out in 1833. Maria was the model for both the lovable but naïve Dora in *David Copperfield*, and – rather damningly, after Dickens met her some twenty years later – for the tiresome, maudlin Flora Finching in *Little Dorrit*. Mr Dorrit's bankers were also in Lombard Street and, looking up, you may notice that the road contains some ancient street signs, belonging to various banks and financial institutions. These include the grasshopper emblem of the family of Thomas Gresham, who founded the first Royal Exchange. These were, however, removed as dangerous hazards, long before Dickens was born, and only restored to the street in 1902 for the coronation of Edward VII.

Cut through Clement's Lane, opposite George Yard, and walk down to King William Street, where you need to turn left. At the end of the road, cross on the right to the far side of Cannon Street, then turn left and then cross over the approach to London Bridge. Turn right, as if heading to cross the bridge, then take a left down Monument Street.

The Monument is a memorial to the Great Fire of London in 1666, designed by Wren and his colleague Dr Robert Hooke, and completed in 1677. It is 202 feet high, which is also the distance between its site and where the Great Fire began in Pudding Lane. It is a hollow column with a spiral staircase leading to a lofty viewing platform. The flaming urn on top has been regilded three times, in 1834, 1954 and 2008. The cage atop the railings is a Victorian addition of the 1840s, following a spate of suicides. It was a tourist attraction for Victorian visitors and it features repeatedly in *Martin Chuzzlewit*: Todgers' lodging house, where the Pecksniffs make their London home, is nearby. Dickens also works a caricature of the 'Man in the Monument' into the novel – the keeper of the building, who 'lived' in the little pay-booth at the bottom of the stairs. This City functionary takes great pleasure in his work. Of unwary visitors, he laughs, 'They don't know what a many steps there is! … It's worth twice the money to stop here. Oh, my eye!'

Continue down Monument Street to Upper Thames Street. Opposite you is Billingsgate Market, the traditional landing place for fish in the City of London. It has been through various incarnations and the present one is post-Dickensian, by City architect Horace Jones, finished in 1875 (Smithfield Market, in Walk 6, was also designed by Jones), and now used as an exhibition and events venue. We can follow the walk on the left-hand side of the market to reach the riverside.

The next building by the river, turning left when you see the Thames, is the Custom House, which, in the nineteenth century, housed about three hundred officials devoted to calculating and collecting customs duties on goods coming into the country, as well

The Monument to the Great Fire of London.

A weathervane at Billingsgate Market.

WALK 8

121

The early-nineteenth-century Embankment by the Custom House.

St Olave's Church, dubbed 'Saint Ghastly Grim' by Dickens.

as many more men on 'out-door work'. Much of this work was in London – about 50 per cent of the duties collected nationally came from the capital's docks. The building was completed in 1817 but, through shoddy workmanship, it was constructed on pilings that rotted, which led to a collapse of part of the famous 'Long Room'. It was, therefore, given a new façade by Robert Smirke in 1825. The building is mentioned in several of Dickens' books, and in *Bleak House* we learn that the once-neglected Peepy Jellyby has found a job here. When the tide is low, you can explore the river here, descending down steps to a beach, where the embankment bears the date of 1819 inscribed into the stonework.

Double back to Lower Thames Street and cross the road, then take the first left up St Dunstan's Hill, where a Blitz-damaged church has been turned into a beautiful public garden. At the top of the hill turn right, then take a left down Mark Lane. This road has an interesting Victorian survival: the office block at 59 Mark Lane with its three storeys of arcaded windows formed of Venetian-Byzantine style arches. It was built as a speculation in 1864 – one of the first purpose-built blocks of lettable offices in London.

Turn right after the office block down Hart Street, then take the next right down Seething Lane. On the right is a sight familiar to Dickens, St Olave's, a medieval church (restored after the Second World War); its distinctive gate is topped with skulls and iron spikes dating to the late seventeenth century. Dickens mentions the church in one of his *Uncommercial Traveller* essays, marvelling at the skeletal adornments, wondering how 'it came into the mind of Saint Ghastly Grim, that to stick iron spikes a-top of the stone skulls, as though they were impaled, would be a pleasant device'.

WALK 8

The Tower of London, seen from the Mint.

Turn left into Pepys Street and right into Savage Gardens. This will bring you to Trinity Square, the site of Trinity House, which stands on your left as you enter the open space. This is the home of the lighthouse authority for England and Wales, a building completed in 1796. It is in the gardens ahead of you that Bella Wilfer of *Our Mutual Friend* tarries a while, before taking her father for a day out in Greenwich.

Trinity House, home of the lighthouse authority (completed 1796).

Beyond those gardens lies the Tower of London, the historic fortress that holds the Crown Jewels. This is another of London's long-standing tourist attractions to which David Copperfield takes Peggotty. The malicious dwarf Quilp of *The Old Curiosity Shop* also lives on Tower Hill, opposite Quilp's Wharf on the south side of the river, with its yard containing 'a few fragments of rusty anchors; several large iron rings; some piles of rotten wood; and two or three heaps of old sheet copper, crumpled, cracked, and battered'.

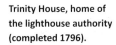

WALK 8

The old Ivory Warehouse in St Katharine's Docks.

Unless you wish to enter the Tower, turn left on to Tower Hill. Cross the Minories, turn right, crossing Shorter Street, then keep going, crossing Mansell Street. Opposite the north-eastern corner of the Tower you will come to East Smithfield and the gateway to the former Royal Mint, built in 1809, although much altered and extended during its lifespan. The last coin was struck here in 1975 (the present-day Mint is in South Wales). The high brick wall surrounding the site is indicative of the prison-like security that once pervaded.

Follow East Smithfield around the corner of the Mint to a pedestrian crossing, which will take you to the other side of East Smithfield and the gate to St Katharine's Docks (also often spelt 'St Katherine's'). The docks were opened in 1828 to handle the increasing amount of shipping coming to London from all corners of the burgeoning British Empire. The narrow quays of the docks are deliberate, with warehouses built close to the water's edge to allow for immediate storage. The docks were converted into a marina and shopping complex in the 1970s. You will see the central Ivory Warehouse immediately ahead of you; true to its name, it would have once dealt exclusively with ivory ('heaps of elephant and rhinoceros tusks, the ivory weapons of sword-fish, &c'), alongside other buildings containing tobacco, spices, ostrich feathers and other more mundane imports. The walk into the docks was not such an easy one in Dickens' day. Dock workers were casual labour, with thousands of men milling outside the gates before dawn, in the hope of catching the eye of a foreman. Many were turned away. Tourists also came to inspect the warehouses but the docks were surrounded by high walls, with strong gates, just like the Mint. Visitors were checked by dock police, like the dockers themselves, to ensure none of the valuable cargoes stored in the great warehouses was pilfered.

Our next part of the walk will take us in a rambling route along the Thames. First you must leave St Katharine's Docks, so look for the peculiar white-pillared building (Tower Walk, a pseudo-Regency oddity from the late 1980s) next to the bridge at the dock entrance, on the far side of the Ivory Warehouse. You may also notice the Dickens Inn to its left, an incongruous modern attempt at recreating a galleried coaching inn from the timbers of an old warehouse – it has no connection with Dickens, beyond being opened by his great-grandson in 1976.

The path to the left of the white 'Regency' house will lead you to St Katharine's Way, with council flats on the left and converted warehouses on the right. We shall now follow the road, as it runs beside the Thames. Once on Wapping High Street, you will see a small

A nineteenth-century overhead view of St Katharine's Docks.

WALK 8

riverside park on the right, next to some bow-fronted modern flats. If you stroll to the river wall, you may just be able to see a narrow inlet next to the large Butler's Wharf warehouses on the other side of the river, with a modern white bridge crossing it. This was once Jacob's Island, the dismal creek where Bill Sikes meets his doom in *Oliver Twist*.

Continue along Wapping High Street. Initially this may appear unpromising. The cobbles belong to Dickens' London but the warehouse conversions are buildings of the late-Victorian era; and some are even pristine and sanitised modern imitations. But keep going until you reach Pier Head, one of London's most remarkable squares – one side of the square being the waterfront. This was once a lock leading to the London Docks (opened 1805), with houses for dock officials built on either side between 1811 and 1813. The canal from the lock and the London Docks themselves were filled in during the 1970s and there is now a private garden in the square. Past the Pier Head, along Wapping High Street, you also increasingly find narrow alleys with sets of steps leading down to the water – these were the old riverside landing places for small boats, where the likes of Gaffer Hexam of *Our Mutual Friend* would have moored. You will also pass the modern headquarters of the Marine Police. Dickens was fascinated by the activity of the police in London and, in 1853, wrote an article in *Household Words* entitled 'Down with the Tide', recounting a night spent on a 'four-oared Thames Police Galley' on the river.

Dock officials' houses at Pier Head, Wapping.

Our walk ends halfway along the High Street at Wapping station. It is the one underground station that we can be fairly sure Dickens knew – after a fashion. For this was another famous Victorian tourist attraction. The current station, on the railway connecting Wapping

WALK 8

and Rotherhithe, was the entrance to the Thames Tunnel, the world's first underwater tunnel, and the steps in the station still line the walls of the tunnel's original cavernous entrance shaft. The tunnel was built by Marc Brunel beneath the river, at a great cost in workers' lives and investors' cash. Work commenced in the 1820s and the venture was not completed until 1843. Even then, there was no money for the planned access ramps for carriages. It remained,

Engraving of the steps leading down to the Thames Tunnel, opened in 1843.

therefore, a gas-lit pedestrian tunnel with a motley collection of sellers of knick-knacks and souvenirs filling the many alcoves between its twin horseshoe-shaped paths. It had a dubious reputation as 'a kind of mouldy and poverty-stricken bazaar'. The tunnel was closed to the public and transferred to the East London Railway in 1865.

RIVERSIDE EXTENSION

If you wish to extend your walk along the river, you can continue towards Dickens' Limehouse. Note that this will add an hour and a half to your walk.

Continue along the remainder of Wapping High Street and, when the road curves to the left, take a right along Wapping Wall. At the end of Wapping Wall is the Prospect of Whitby public house, originally built in 1520. Dickens is reputed to have been a customer here, and the wood-panelled interior certainly preserves the maritime atmosphere of old Wapping.

Go past the Prospect of Whitby, and just after the bridge to Shadwell Basin (an extension to the London Docks which has outlived its original purpose) take a right turn along an alley by the recreation ground. This will lead you to the King Edward Memorial Park on the edge of the river, which will eventually bring you out to Narrow Street, behind more riverside flats. Look out for Limehouse Basin on

WALK 8

The Prospect of Whitby
public house, exterior
and interior.

Mid-Victorian warehouse
at Dunbar Wharf,
Limehouse.

WALK 8

your left – built to link the Regent's Canal with the Thames, opened in 1820. Then, a little further on, you will pass a small public house on the right, the Grapes (opposite Brightlingsea Place and the evocatively named Ropemakers' Fields). This is the undisputed original of the 'Six Jolly Fellowship Porters', the 'tavern of a dropsical appearance' in *Our Mutual Friend.*

Follow Narrow Street as it curves around to the left. You will see Dunbar Wharf on your right, a set of mid-Victorian warehouses, on a smaller scale than the later warehouses of Wapping, and more typical of Dickens' London. We shall come back to them, but first continue and take a left down Three Colts Street. This will take you through modern council estates, under the Docklands Light Railway, to St Anne's, Limehouse.

It was at this magnificent Hawksmoor church (built 1712–24) that Miss Potterson, mistress of the Six Jolly Fellowship Porters, was christened. But, more significantly, if you leave the churchyard by the principal entrance on the western side, you will come out on Newell Street, formerly Church Row. Here at No. 5 was the home of Christopher Huffam, Dickens' godfather and a local sailmaker, which Dickens often visited as a boy – his first acquaintance with maritime London.

Retrace your steps to the Dunbar Wharf warehouses and look for a walkway between the modern flats immediately after them, which will take you back out on to a riverside walk. On your left is Limekiln Dock, an eighteenth-century dock, and the river-front of the Dunbar Wharf warehouses we just passed. You are now in the district that was once known as Limehouse Hole. Rogue Riderhood in *Our Mutual Friend* lives in this area. It is also the 'old neighbourhood' of the well-meaning Captain Cuttle in *Dombey and Son*, 'down among the mast, oar, and block makers, ship-biscuit bakers, coal-whippers, pitch-kettles, sailors, canals, docks, swing-bridges, and other soothing objects'.

To find any more of Dickens' Limehouse is a tricky business. The best plan is to continue a short way along the riverside to the steps up to Westferry Circus, in the heart of the new Docklands. Walk straight ahead down West India Avenue, then take a left at Cabot Square. This will take you over a bridge to West India Quay. No. 1 and No. 2 Warehouse, in the row facing you, are among the oldest warehouses in the country, built together with the docks between 1800 and 1804. They also house the excellent Museum of London Docklands, which includes, among other things, 'Sailortown', an authentic recreation of the early-nineteenth-century riverside, including a typical small beer shop – except, of course, no alcohol is available. For that, you may wish to return to the Grapes, or to restaurants and bars conveniently adjacent to the museum.

A recreation of nineteenth-century Wapping at the Museum of London Docklands.

WALK 8

FOCUS ON: *THE LONDON DOCKS*

The London Docks were the second great enclosed dock to be built east of the Tower of London. The West India Docks were finished in 1802; the London Docks in 1805. Access was from the south, from a channel beginning at what is now Pier Head Square. Shadwell Basin was built in the late 1820s, and a second, eastern entrance was constructed. The latter, together with the basin, still survives. It can be seen just after the Prospect of Whitby, if you follow the extension to the riverside walk. Building these docks was a monumental task. The site was 90 acres, only 35 of which was water – the rest was quays, jetties and warehouses – all surrounded by an unscalable high wall. The quays could cope with three hundred vessels; the buildings could accommodate 220,000 tons of goods; vast underground vaults could store thousands of barrels of wine, sherry, brandy and rum. Wine vaults were a particular tourist attraction, for obvious reasons ('Those wishing to taste the wines must obtain a tasting order from a wine merchant. Ladies are not admitted after 1 p.m.').

The district surrounding the docks also appealed to visitors, with its distinctly maritime air. Ship's instruments, ropes and hammocks hung in windows; pawnshops were filled with a selection of quadrants, sextants, chronometers and mariner's compasses; clothes shops specialised in 'nor'westers' or 'sou'westers' (no discernible

Ostrich feathers in a warehouse at the London Docks.

difference between the two), pilot coats, canvas trousers, or the parti-coloured shirts supposedly beloved by the proverbial 'jolly tar'. Customs officials were omnipresent, with their distinctive brass-buttoned uniforms. This was, moreover, the one part of London in which nobody thought it unusual to see Africans or Asians. Wapping not only looked different, it had a distinctive sound: the rattle of chains as cranes winched their cargoes from the holds; the rumbling of empty casks on cobbled streets; the jumble of the sailors' different mother tongues. The docks also lent a unique aroma, according to what ship had just berthed, from pungent tobacco to the dizzying fumes of rum.

Various maritime businesses thrived in the district – the ships' outfitters, ropemakers and so on – but the docks also provided more unusual commercial opportunities. The strangest warehouse in Wapping belonged not to a tobacco dealer or wine merchant, but to a certain Mr Jamrach. He was a dealer in wild animals, based in Old Gravel Lane, which ran between the buildings of the London Docks. He supplied captains of merchant ships with a 'priced list of animals' and his agents would, in turn, board incoming ships and enquire if they had any finds. In one transaction, a canny merchant seaman could make more than a year's pay. Jamrach, in turn, sold birds and beasts to zoos and private menageries, not only in Britain but throughout the British Empire and across the globe. Indian princes were said to be particularly interested in collecting exotic beasts. Mr Jamrach's curious stock varied, but his rates in the 1870s were: zebras £100 to £150 each; camels £20; giraffes £40; ostriches £80; polar bears £25; other bears from £8 to £16; leopards £20; lions £100; tigers £300.

JACOB'S ISLAND

From *Oliver Twist*

To reach this place, the visitor has to penetrate through a maze of close, narrow, and muddy streets, thronged by the roughest and poorest of waterside people, and devoted to the traffic they may be supposed to occasion. The cheapest and least delicate provisions are heaped in the shops; the coarsest and commonest articles of wearing apparel dangle at the salesman's door, and stream from the house-parapet and windows. Jostling with unemployed labourers of the lowest class, ballast-heavers, coal-whippers, brazen women, ragged children, and the raff and refuse of the river, he makes his way with difficulty along, assailed by offensive sights and smells from the narrow alleys which branch off on the right and left, and deafened by the clash of ponderous waggons that bear great piles of merchandise from the stacks of warehouses that rise from every corner. Arriving, at length, in streets remoter and less-frequented than those through which he has passed, he walks beneath tottering house-

WALK 8

Bill Sikes faces death in Jacob's Island.

fronts projecting over the pavement, dismantled walls that seem to totter as he passes, chimneys half crushed half hesitating to fall, windows guarded by rusty iron bars that time and dirt have almost eaten away, every imaginable sign of desolation and neglect.

In such a neighbourhood, beyond Dockhead in the Borough of Southwark, stands Jacob's Island, surrounded by a muddy ditch, six or eight feet deep and fifteen or twenty wide when the tide is in, once called Mill Pond, but known in the days of this story as Folly Ditch. It is a creek or inlet from the Thames, and can always be filled at high water by opening the sluices at the Lead Mills from which it took its old name. At such times, a stranger, looking from one of the wooden bridges thrown across it at Mill Lane, will see the inhabitants of the houses on either side lowering from their back doors and windows, buckets, pails, domestic utensils of all kinds, in which to haul the water up; and when his eye is turned from these operations to the houses themselves, his utmost astonishment will be excited by the scene before him. Crazy wooden galleries common to the backs of half a dozen houses, with holes from which to look upon the slime beneath; windows, broken and patched, with poles thrust out, on which to dry the linen that is never there; rooms so small, so filthy, so confined, that the air would seem too tainted even for the dirt and squalor which they shelter; wooden chambers thrusting themselves out above the mud, and threatening to fall into it – as some have done; dirt-besmeared walls and decaying foundations; every repulsive lineament of poverty, every loathsome indication of filth, rot, and garbage; all these ornament the banks of Folly Ditch.

In Jacob's Island, the warehouses are roofless and empty; the walls are crumbling down; the windows are windows no more; the doors are falling into the streets; the chimneys are blackened, but they yield no smoke. Thirty or forty years ago, before losses and chancery suits came upon it, it was a thriving place; but now it is a desolate island indeed. The houses have no owners; they are broken open, and entered upon by those who have the courage; and there they live, and there they die. They must have powerful motives for a secret residence, or be reduced to a destitute condition indeed, who seek a refuge in Jacob's Island.

WALK 8

INDEX

*Page numbers in italics
refer to illustrations*

59 Mark Lane 122
A Christmas Carol 119
A Tale of Two Cities 29,
  46, 49, 68, 94
Adelaide Gallery 53
Adelphi 43, *43*, *44*
Albany, The 15
All the Year Round 35, 41
Apsley House 19
Athenaeum Club 12, *12*
Bank of England 117, *118*
Barnaby Rudge 47, 106
Barnards' Inn 81, 84
Barrow, Thomas Culliford
  26
Battle Bridge 67
Bayham Street 5
Bazalgette, Joseph 40, *41*
Beadnell, Maria 120
Bell Yard 74
Bentinck Street 18
Berry Bros & Rudd 13
Billingsgate Market 121,
  121
Bleak House 10, 26, 53,
  59, 63, *63*, 69–70, 73,
  74, 76, 77, *77*, 81,
  87, 103, 105, 122
Bleeding Hart Yard 81
Borough Market 106, *106*,
  111
Bow Street 35
British Museum 59–60
Broad Street pump 28, *28*

Buckingham Street 42
Burlington Arcade 15–16,
  16, 19–20
Burlington House 15
Carlton House Terrace 11
Cavendish Square 17–18
Charing Cross 52
Charterhouse Street
  86–7, 91, *91*
Cheapside 116
Clerkenwell Green 92–5,
  94, *95*
Cleveland Street Work-
  house 58
Cleveland Street 57–8
Clifford's Inn 71, *73*
Clink Prison 106
College of Arms, The *104*
Collins, Wilkie 24, 62
Cornhill 119
Court for the Relief of
  Insolvent Debtors 75
Covent Garden 19, 32–7
Covent Garden Theatre 35
Custom House 121–2, *122*
Davey, Robert 59
David Copperfield 26, 27,
  34, 41, 46, 48, 51,
  59, 62, *63*, 76, 79,
  82, 103, 104–5
Dickens Coffee House 35
Dickens House Museum
  62, *62*
Dickens, John 4–5, 44,
  56, 59, 108
Doctor Johnson's House
  49

Doctor's Commons 5,
  104, *105*
Dodd, John 58
Dolby, George 20
Dombey and Son 18,
  118, *119*
Doughty Street 62
Duke of York's Column
  11, *11*
Duke's Road 65, 65
Dunbar Wharf 128, *128*
Edwin Drood 79, *79*, 99
Egyptian Hall 20
Ellis & Blackmore 78
Ely Place *81*, 82
Euston Station 65–6, *66*
Exeter Hall 53
Field Lane 87
Fitzroy Square *56*
Fitzroy Street 56
Fleet Street *51*
Floral Hall, Covent Garden
  35
Forster, John 76, *76*
Foundling Hospital 61–2
Fountain Court, Temple
  47, 54–5
Frozen Deep, The 24
Furnival's Inn 80, *82*
Garden Court, Temple 47
Garrick Club 32
General Post Office 99,
  101
George and Vulture Chop
  House 119
George Inn 108, *109*
Gerrard Street 26

Golden Cross 51
Golden Square 26
Gower Street North 56
Grapes pub 128
Gray's Inn 5, 78–9, *78*
Great Expectations 27, 34,
    47, 81, 90, 105, 116
Guy's Hospital 107, *107*
Hanover Square Rooms 17
Harley Street 18, 21
Hatton Garden 82–83
Haymarket 23–6, *23*
Haymarket Theatre 6,
    23–5
Her Majesty's Theatre
    23–4
Hogarth, Catherine 62
Holborn Hill *85*
Holborn Viaduct 85–7, *88*
Holywell Street 45, 53
Horse Guards 9–10, *11*
Horsemonger Lane gaol
    112
Hospital for Sick Children
    61, *61*
House of Charity 29
Household Words 61–2,
    126
Huffam, Christopher 128
Hungerford Bridge 40
Hungerford Market 42, 52
Jacob's Island 126, 131–3
James Smith & Son
    Umbrellas 60, *60*
Jermyn Street 14
Jerusalem Tavern 92, *93*
Jerrold, Douglas 24
John Soane House 76
Johnson's Court 50
Keppel Street 59
King's Bench gaol 112
Law Society 73–4, *74*
Leather Lane 80, 82–83,

83
Leicester Square 26
Limekiln Dock 129
Lincoln's Inn 76–7, *77*, *78*
Lincoln's Inn Fields 75–76
Linwood's Exhibition 26
Little Dorrit 18, 34, 44,
    46, 62, 72, 75, 79, 90,
    99, 106, 109–12, *110*
Lock & Co 13, *14*
Lombard Street 120
London Bridge Station 111
London Docks 126,
    130–1
London Homoeopathic
    Hospital 61
London Transport Museum
    34
Lowther Arcade 52
Manette Street 29
Mansion House 117, *118*
Marshalsea gaol 6,
    109–113
Martin Chuzzlewit 10,
    34, 47, 54–5, 81,
    90, 99, 121
Marx Memorial Library
    93, *93*
Meard Street *28*
Metropolitan Board of
    Works 29, 40
Metropolitan Drinking
    Fountain Association 88,
    89, 93, *95*
Middlesex Hospital 57, *58*
Midland Grand Hotel 7,
    64, *64*
Middlesex Sessions House
    93, *94*
Monthly Magazine 5, 49
Monument, The 120–1,
    121
Morning Chronicle 5

Mrs Lirriper's Lodgings 46
Mrs Salmon's Waxworks
    48
Museum of London Dock-
    lands 129, *129*
Mystery of Edwin Drood, The
    41
Newgate gaol 88–9,
    96–8, *97*
Newell Street 128
Newman Passage *58*, 59
Nicholas Nickleby 5, *17*, 18,
    27, 31, 59, 62, *88*, 99,
    103, 112, 119–20
Night Walks 37
No Thoroughfare 62
Old Curiosity Shop 113,
    117, 123
Old Curiosity Shop
    (building) 75
Old Operating Theatre
    Museum 107, *108*
Olde Cheshire Cheese, Ye
    49, *49*
Olde Mitre, Ye 81, *81*
Oliver Twist 5, 57, 62,
    87, 90, 94, *95*, 126,
    131–3, *132*
On Duty with Inspector Field
    31
Our Mutual Friend 12, 14,
    18, 41, 47, 68, 72, 94,
    106, 123, 126, 128–9
Pall Mall 11–12
Palmerston, Lord 13
Paternoster Square 101–2
Paxton & Whitfield 14, *14*
Pier Head Square 126,
    126
Piccadilly 14–15
Pickering Place 13, *14*
Pickwick Papers, The 5,
    44, 51, 62, 72, 75, 77,

79, 90, 104, 107–8, 110, 111, 119, 120
Pier Head Square 126, *126*
Prince Henry's Room 47–8, *48*
Printing House Square 104
Prospect of Whitby pub 127, *128*
Public Records Offce 73, *74*
Quin, Frederic Hervey Foster 61
Regent's Canal 67, *67*, 68
Resurrection gate 30, *30*
Roman Baths 45, *46*
Rothschild, Walter 19
Rowland Hill 101, *101*
Royal Academy 15, 20, *15*
Royal College of Surgeons 75
Royal Courts of Justice, The 74
Royal Exchange 118, *119*
Royal Mint 124
Royal Opera House 35, *35*
RSA 43
Rules Restaurant 33, *33*
Saffron Hill 87
Savile Row 16
Serjeant's Inn 72, *73*
Seven Dials 30–1, *31*, 38
Simpson's Chop House 119, *120*
Sketches by Boz 5, 30, 38–9, 96–8
Smithfield 89–91, *90*, *92*
Snow, John 27–8
Somerset House 44–5, *45*
Southwark Bridge 106
St Alban The Martyr church 83

St Andrew-by-the-Wardrobe 103–4, *104*
St Andrew's Gardens 62–3, *62*
St Anne's church, Limehouse 128
St Bartholomew's Hospital 90, *90*
St Bartholomew the Great church 90, *91*
St Clement Danes church 46, 53
St Dunstan's-in-the-West church 49, *49*, 71
St George's church, Bloomsbury Way 60, *60*
St George's church, Hanover Square 16–17
St George-the-Martyr church 109–10, *110*
St Giles-in-the-Fields church 29–30, *31*
St James's church, Piccadilly 14, *15*
St James's Hall 20
St James's Park 10–11, *10*
St John's Gate 92, *92*
St Katharine's Docks 124–5, *124–5*
St Martin's-le-Grand 99
St Mary-le-Bow church 116–117
St Mary-le-Strand church 45, 53
St Olave's church 122, *122*
St Pancras New Church 64–65, *65*
St Pancras Old Church 68
St Paul's Cathedral 102–3, *103*, 105, *105*, 115
St Paul's church, Covent Garden 32, 37

St Sepulchre's church 89, *89*
Staple Inn 79, *79*, *80*
Star Yard 74
Stationer's Hall 103, *103*
Strand, The 44–5, 51–3, *52*
Sweeney Todd 49
Temple 46–7, *47–8*
Temple Bar 46, 102, *102*
Ternan, Ellen 24, 32
Thackeray, William Makepeace 32
Thames Tunnel 127, *127*
Tower of London 123, *123*
Trafalgar Square 52
Traveller's Club 11
Trinity House 123, *123*
Uncommercial Traveller, The 122
Victoria Embankment Gardens 42
Wallace Collection 18–19
Warren's blacking factory 5, 32–3, *33*
Waterloo Place *13*
West, Charles 61
White Hart coaching inn 113–4, *114*
Yates, Edmund 32
York Water Gate 42, *42*